fearless

Also by Jelena Dokic

Unbreakable (with Jessica Halloran)

fearless

finding the power to thrive

JELENA DOKIC

with Jessica Halloran

VIKING
an imprint of
PENGUIN BOOKS

VIKING

UK | USA | Canada | Ireland | Australia
India | New Zealand | South Africa | China

Viking is part of the Penguin Random House group of companies
whose addresses can be found at global.penguinrandomhouse.com

Penguin
Random House
Australia

First published by Viking in 2023

Cover photography by Julian Kingma
Cover design by Adam Laszczuk © Penguin Random House Australia Pty Ltd
Internal design by Midland Typesetters, Australia
Typeset in 12.5/18 pt Minion Pro by Midland Typesetters

Printed and bound in Australia by Griffin Press, an accredited
ISO AS/NZS 14001 Environmental Management Systems printer

A catalogue record for this
book is available from the
NATIONAL LIBRARY OF AUSTRALIA   National Library of Australia

ISBN 978 0 14377 729 8

penguin.com.au

MIX
Paper | Supporting
responsible forestry
FSC® C018684

*We at Penguin Random House Australia acknowledge that Aboriginal and Torres Strait Islander
peoples are the Traditional Custodians and the first storytellers of the lands on which we live
and work. We honour Aboriginal and Torres Strait Islander peoples' continuous connection to
Country, waters, skies and communities. We celebrate Aboriginal and Torres Strait Islander
stories, traditions and living cultures; and we pay our respects to Elders past and present.*

CONTENTS

To my readers, my supporters, my community,
thank you for everything.
And to anyone who is struggling in their lives –
this book is for you.
I hope my story and my words give you strength and hope.

Prologue

FEARLESS

Don't you dare say anything to anyone.
Don't you dare say anything because I will kill you.

These were the words repeated to me almost daily by my father. For decades I lived under his rules, even after I had escaped his physical and verbal abuse. And his number one rule was to be, and to stay, silent. I feared that I would lose my life if I spoke out.

Evil festers in the darkness, in the silence and in the secrets we are forced to keep by our abusers.

So for years I barely told a soul the truth. I lived in perpetual fear.

I am writing this book, my second, to talk about the power of truth-telling, the power of sharing your story, the power of speaking up. I am here for all of you who are yet to find your voice, and to give hope to those who have suffered or are going through difficult moments.

I am here to tell you, you are not alone.

When I was writing my first book, *Unbreakable*, I still had so much fear, shame and embarrassment around the abuse I had endured. There was – and I would say there still is – a stigma around talking about abuse. At that time, few had spoken up about the toxic culture of abuse that lies deep in the tennis world, even in sport and society in general.

There was also stigma and shame associated with talking about mental health, bullying, family violence, body issues (anything that does not resemble society's idea of ideal).

Things have changed since then – not least there's been the #MeToo movement – but at the same time I would say much more can be done and must be done to make a difference. This is why I am writing my second book.

This book is about finding your voice, your power, and thriving. It's about normalising the conversation around many very important issues because that is where change starts – by sharing our stories and speaking up without shame.

This book is about surviving the pain of my childhood and finding hope.

In the following pages I am going to open up about some of my worst moments not only of the last five years, but also in parts of my life I had long buried and hadn't dealt with until relatively recently.

In each chapter you will read about my deepest feelings and experiences; of moments I have never spoken about – and what I have learnt to get through my hardships and heal.

When I was going through some of these most difficult moments, I felt like there wasn't really a person I could look to and think, yeah, they've been through what I have been through, but they are still fulfilling their dreams and goals. So I want to be a voice for women, men, boys and girls – anyone who is not living the life they deserve to live. It's about not letting others silence us, take away our voice and happiness when these were never theirs to take.

It took me some time to get to this place, that is to know my purpose. To be honest, ten years ago I had no real idea what I was going to do with my life. When I first retired from tennis, I found myself in the pits of depression quickly and suddenly. I was, I can see in hindsight, a traumatised young woman with little to aspire to, having been forced to leave the game I loved, the career I loved.

I was wading through life with sadness. I struggled with friendships so my circle was small. My self-worth was shot. My eating became horribly disordered. I didn't want to leave my apartment, and a feeling of hopelessness engulfed my life (not for the first time).

My dark secrets were deep. I had touched on the carnage of my youth with only a very few people. It was not until the spring of 2016, when I decided to write *Unbreakable*, that I started (and the emphasis is on 'start') to process for the first time the gravity of the abuse I'd lived with for many years.

I felt so much shame and I carried it in my body and soul. It was killing me on the inside.

But somewhere in me, I still had a flicker of fight and hence I found the bravery to tell my story.

I remember the morning I sat down in the meeting room of my Melbourne apartment block and started to talk and talk, cry, and talk some more to Jess, who was helping me write *Unbreakable*. I had never told my story in full, not even to my then long-time partner Tin.

Writing that book was tough. I would fall into bed exhausted most nights. But I had no idea at the time how therapeutic it would be for me. The interviews and writing unlocked a lot of difficult feelings, thoughts and stories I had kept firmly inside. Stirring up so many memories triggered panic attacks and terrible fear; for example, that I was being watched and stalked as I walked around Melbourne's CBD.

I was utterly relieved when we submitted the final manuscript to Penguin. Then I felt fear. To be frank, I realised that a lot of shit was going to be put out in public, and I felt extremely vulnerable. I had a deep concern, too: I knew my story was inflammatory, on many levels. This was pre #MeToo – the world much less an environment where survivors' stories were heard and believed. I wondered if people were going to understand me. And I have to make it clear that I wasn't really conscious of the power that telling my story would have not only on my life but on other people's. Did I hope it might help someone else? Absolutely. But as I was writing the book I would often wonder out loud if anyone would actually buy it.

———————

The day Unbreakable *came out was literally one of the best days of my life.*

———————

Finally, the truth was out and I felt like tons of weight had been lifted off my shoulders – a truckload of emotional baggage that I didn't even realise was there.

The book appeared on the front page of almost every newspaper in Australia. It was the lead story on the news all around Australia. As it played out on a bulletin, I was on the phone to a friend. I actually gasped at the vision of my father being crazy at the US Open and Wimbledon, and I remember telling my friend at the end of the segment, 'When I see it all packaged up like that, I start to realise that what I lived with was a *lot* of shit. He was really crazy.'

People had told me it would cause a stir in Australia – anything to do with my father stirred the media – but the reverberations of my graphic account of his abuse also made international headlines. CNN reported, 'Jelena Dokic details claims of years of abuse by her father'; ESPN wrote, 'Retired tennis player Jelena Dokic details alleged abuse by father'; and other websites led with headlines like 'Jelena Dokic was beaten unconscious by her own father'. A few months later the book was published in the States and the *New York Times* wrote, 'Jelena Dokic recounts her rise in tennis with an abusive father'.

So as the book launched around the world, two things were happening. People reacted to the truth with so much support, and for the first time I started to grasp the trauma I was living with and the impact it was having on my life, as well as the impact sharing it was having on others.

At that time, there were still many emotions buried inside of me. There was the relief I've described, the positivity of having taken this step. However, even though I had released the facts of my story to the world, I was yet to fully process what I had been through. There's a passage in the book *The Body Keeps the Score* that rings true to me:

> While we all want to move beyond trauma, the part of our brain that is devoted to ensuring our survival (deep below our rational brain) is not very good at denial. Long after a traumatic experience is over, it may be reactivated at the slightest hint of danger and mobilize disturbed brain circuits and secrete massive amounts of stress hormones.

While I had escaped my family home many moons before 2017, and had given up the fruitless task of trying to repair my relationship with my father, I was struggling, but I wasn't aware of why, or of what was triggering me. And often it was little things. Once, when Tin raised his hand to his head to brush away his hair, I ducked. It was a physical response I had to years of my father hitting me. I was used to 'getting hit', kicked, punched. I just lived like this – with that pain of my childhood, my youth buried very deep. So, yes, on a superficial level my story was out there in the world, it was factual, it was the truth, my lived experience – but had I dealt with the trauma? No. Let's just put that in capitals: NO.

I'll be coming back to this trauma, and how I'm coming to terms with it, but what I realised after the truth-telling was that sharing stories not only brings out secrets from the dark into the relief of the light, but it also connects us to other people, and this is exactly what my father didn't want for me.

He wanted to keep me to himself. Remember, one of his rules was that I wasn't to have friends.

While I was taught as a little girl to say nothing, as a woman no one could stop me from stepping into my power and raising up my voice. And as people read the book and reacted to it, I began to discover the importance of speaking up.

The first time that truly dawned on me was on my book tour. It was late November 2017 and we were at an RSL club in Maroochydore on the Sunshine Coast of Queensland. As people packed the room, there was a buzz of excitement. I was interviewed, I told my story, speaking from the heart.

Afterwards, people came up to talk to me. Some expressed their shock about what I had survived. One woman pulled me quietly to the side to tell me of the domestic violence she had suffered – and was still suffering. She poured out her heart – how she was still in that situation, she was still trying to find the strength to leave. She said she had read my book and it had given her some fortitude and the hope of a better life.

It was then, in that moment, that it was confirmed to me that the purpose of my story, my truth, my life so far, was about giving at the very least one person hope.

I've had thousands of similar conversations since. People – and while it is usually women, there have certainly been men who speak to me as well – in the audience at book signings, at keynote presentations, DM'ing me: 'You make me feel like

I'm not alone in my struggles.' 'Thank you for being so open and vulnerable and giving me a voice.' 'What you've gone through has given me strength to know I can get through.'

Sometimes people stop me in the street. One day I heard someone calling to me at a set of traffic lights near the Botanic Gardens in Melbourne. I was standing at the crossing waiting for the light to turn green, and all of a sudden I saw a car window wind down and there was a woman hanging out of it. She was furiously waving, then she shouted, 'Oh my god! I love you! My mum loves you! My friends love you! Thank you so much for telling your story.'

To have people respond like this, and know that hearing my story helps them, drives me to keep going. That's why I speak at events, on social media, on other media platforms. It's a great feeling to know I can do a little bit of good and change something out of what was such a bad situation.

So these coming pages are a confessional of sorts, but with a purpose, because toxic secrecy continues to swirl around all the subjects I will talk about. And I want to fight that secrecy, shake the silence and the shackles around talking about these issues, keep on elevating them so we can find a way through. There's so much power in storytelling, so much strength in sharing. If we voice these things, we no longer surrender control to our abusers; we no longer bottle up our most difficult moments. I feel like I have regained control by talking about what I have been through; that I have had an evolution of sorts. I have grown and I am still growing to this day.

Writing the words in this book has helped me to come to better understand my mental health and how to take care of it properly for the first time ever in my life. They are about me finding my self-worth. But most of all, I am telling my story candidly so I can hopefully inspire and empower people who may be struggling to make that first important step to speak to friends, family or a professional.

As I write, I have been dealing with the enormous emotional toll of a break-up with the love of my life. I am alone – truly alone – for the first time since I escaped my family unit one night in Moscow when I was nineteen. The demise of this relationship left me suicidal, and I will talk about how the darkness engulfed me . . . but also how I found my light. Because the only silver lining from the break-up with my partner of nineteen years is that it pushed me into therapy properly for the first time in my life. For a long time I didn't even know that professional help was an option and I certainly didn't realise how much it could help me.

On my thirty-ninth birthday, when a close friend asked what I was doing for the day, I said, 'Um . . . talking with my psychiatrist.' We both burst out laughing at the dark humour of it all. That would be right for me – spending a good chunk of my birthday talking to my shrink. And yet I was so happy to do that. It's what I need, it's what helps me maintain some equilibrium, and it's what helps me deeply make myself better.

I have to say, dark humour also helps me through – actually laughing at the ridiculously bad things, I think this is a strength of mine; an ability to somehow see the light in the darkest times of life.

So I have decided to delve into these corners of my life, going deeper into how the trauma of my childhood and youth manifested – but most importantly, how I am getting through it. And I hope that reading about this may encourage you to get professional help, if you think you need it; to escape, gather strength or to simply be inspired in some way to live better.

If you haven't suffered, maybe these stories will give you an insight into people you know who have had difficult pasts; why we find it hard to trust, and live with sometimes crippling anxiety, or depression, or post-traumatic stress disorder (PTSD), or why we suffer suicidal thoughts or disordered eating. Please don't judge us, but try and understand in order to help us.

The trauma you go through does remain part of you. It's a scar and you don't have to 'get over it'. I don't think I will ever get *over* what I have been through. But I won't be defined by it; I am now determined to grow from it and to be stronger and wiser because of it.

I can't go back and erase the beatings I endured for failing in my father's eyes; that is, as he saw it, not practising hard enough, not playing well enough, or losing. I can't erase the shame I felt when he made me strip down to my sports bra and then proceeded to hit me with a belt to the point of me bleeding. Or when he humiliated me publicly, or when he beat me unconscious. But I am a survivor and I am determined to not be defined by the saddest chapters of my life. And I have made it my mission in this book to be as authentic as possible – scars and all; unafraid to show frailer sides of myself.

As an elite athlete, you have to be a little bit selfish to be the best, and this ability to be focused on yourself can reap you enormous results. It took me to world No. 4 and won me

Women's Tennis Association (WTA) titles. But in my fortieth year on this earth, I am focusing on how I want to live.

Know this: I am not fully healed. I have not fully recovered. I am a work in progress. But I am a fighter.

I want this to be a book you pick up when you are going through a hard time – but this is not a self-help book. And please remember: while I was good with a tennis racquet, I am not in any sense a qualified counsellor so I advise you to seek advice from a professional if you are suffering. Some truly great mental health professionals saved my life, several times. I want to make a point I am not a psychologist, psychiatrist or a mental health expert – these are just my personal experiences and lessons.

I grew up with an idea of who I wanted to be but I became lost. Now I am finding who I, Jelena Dokic, am and want to be.

Please join me on my journey.

Love,
Jelena x

1.

THE POWER OF
SPEAKING UP

I know telling and sharing my story is powerful.
Not only for myself but for other survivors.

Speaking the truth

Experts say that the average victim of abuse takes around twenty-four years to reveal what they've been through, and that while disclosure can never erase what happened, it can be the first step towards healing.

For years I barely told a soul the truth. I was raised to say nothing, to keep secrets, to trust absolutely no one. I was controlled to within an inch of my life. I knew too early it was best not to share any hurt I was feeling.

The secrets began when my father started hitting me. That happened when I first learnt to play tennis as a six-year-old.

You have to understand that from the very beginning tennis gave me joy and satisfaction. I loved it. The tennis court was the place I felt most happiness. But as much as I loved the game from when I first hit a ball as a child, it was then that I also started experiencing immense pressure and abuse from my father.

If you are unfamiliar with my story, my father wanted me to be a tennis player, and it was a Yugoslavian tennis prodigy who triggered him to put a racquet in my hand. That player? Monica Seles. He watched her competing in the 1989 French Open semi-final. Seles lost to Steffi Graf that day, but she sparked something in my father's head.

That year opened a particularly brilliant period for Seles; it was her breakout year. At the time Steffi Graf had been the dominant player in women's tennis, etching herself into the record books. But after 1989 Seles dominated. In March 1991 she stamped her mark on women's tennis. She dethroned Graf as the world No. 1, and won three grand slams that year: the Australian, French and US Opens. My father was inspired. I also admired Monica and Steffi. I liked their humility, their competitive spirit, their intensity and the way they carried themselves. They were incredible players.

One thing was clear to my father: he imagined I could be just like them.

Many years later, I read that Monica Seles's father, Károly, had, like my father, helped to coach her. She told the *Guardian*'s Tim Adams in 2009: 'My dad, as an artist, was aware of the dangers of too much structure; in particular he was very keen that I should not lose my childish imagination when I was playing.' So Károly would draw cartoon faces onto the tennis balls and Seles would aim for those faces.

Károly and Monica's mother, Esther, were in the crowd the day their daughter beat her idol Graf in the 1992 French Open final, and you can see both parents were overcome with joy and tears. It's clear they were a loving family unit.

As you know, things were different in my house. There were no cartoon faces on tennis balls. Tennis was not a place for 'fun', or smiling, or having a good time. From the moment I began playing, my father's rules were about winning at all costs.

'Hard work will make you a champion, Jelena,' he told me often. And you know what, I liked hard work, I still love to work hard, I never feared working my heart out. I would hit in the winter, when there was a thin layer of snow on the roads as we took the tram to the local courts. We lived in a city in Croatia called Osijek, where in the months around Christmas the temperature would frequently dip to -10°C. The cold air would be stinging my cheeks. My father would have his laundry basket of balls on the ground and he would feed them to me. There would be no one else around in these difficult conditions. But with gloves and coats on, cold to my bones, I would practise no matter what.

Even though the conditions were harsh, the training was tough, the pressure was on, I didn't mind because from the moment I picked up a racquet I loved hitting balls, I loved tennis, I loved competing.

With the joy I took in playing, however, came emotional and physical pain. Let's call it for what it is: abuse.

Family is supposed to be our safe space, our support system, our loving home, but it can be a place of the deepest pain and secrets.

My father never physically abused me until I played tennis. I had never been in serious trouble with him until I played tennis. One of the first times my father lashed out at me was during a practice session while he was feeding me balls. He wasn't happy about the fact I couldn't return straight to his hand, so he removed his shoe, came over to me and hit me on the head with it again and again.

Another time, he observed me laughing and joking with my coach after a session. As I walked off the court, my father's face was filled with anger. He told me I had let him down – that tennis was not for fun. He made me do laps of the park as punishment. For fifteen minutes I ran hard, and then we took the tram home in silence. In the lift to the apartment he started yelling at me again, screaming, telling me how hopeless I was. When we got home his rage peaked. He slapped me. His huge right hand struck my six-year-old cheek three times.

I was in shock. As he walked out of the apartment I ran to the phone and called my mum at her work, crying. But he found me doing this and yelled at me to hang up.

It was in that moment that everything changed for me. I realised then that I was not to tell anyone, not to cry to anyone about what he had inflicted on me. Not even my mother. It set the tone: be silent or else. It was the first unwritten rule of my life; my first false belief: I must keep secrets, I must not share the truth with anyone.

Abusers thrive in silence

As the years rolled on, the abuse from my father became more severe and bruises started to appear. He made sure I wore long-sleeved tops to school and training to cover up the marks he had left: those deep-blue, purple bruises on the tops of my arms, welts on my back caused by his belt – all of this reminded me of his anger.

I never wanted to look at these wounds, but sometimes I dared myself to find a mirror and see what he had done to me. When bruises appeared on my body that I couldn't cover up, I would make up a story – that I had fallen over, down the stairs. There was no choice but to lie. It was rare that anyone at school or tennis asked about the marks, but one day he realised it was not possible to miss the physical signs of his abuse. He'd hit me, missed the side of my head and caught my left eye. It went black, blue and purple. My father hid me away that time. I missed training for three days. I missed school.

My entire childhood and youth, until I left home at nineteen, was defined by abuse. I was slapped, spat at, punched, shins kicked, knocked out cold. And then there was the emotional abuse. From the age of twelve I was called a 'whore', a 'bitch', a 'cow' and other vile names. The scars left by the emotional abuse were as bad as the ones left by the physical assaults.

My father instilled in me an expectation – or really it was a rule – to be silent. He wanted me to trust only him. I know now this is the way abusers often operate. Somehow, my father framed that everyone was against me and him. He wanted me to believe the way he treated me was the only way. Also, I knew that if I was to speak about the pain he was inflicting on me, he would seriously harm me.

In Jess Hill's book *See What You Made Me Do*, on domestic violence, abusers and victims, she has a chapter titled 'Children' and in it is a quote from Maya Angelou, American poet and civil rights activist: 'There is no greater agony than bearing an untold story inside you.'

Being abused and living in silence is painful and toxic. Jess Hill's chapter on children who are brought up suffering or watching domestic violence has horrific stories of the impact this has on children. A passage on how, as a child, you try to survive a violent household spoke to me: 'Children trapped in abusive environments have to develop their own strategies to survive – not just physically, but psychologically.' Hill quotes an American psychiatrist who says:

These children must find a way to preserve a sense of trust in people who are untrustworthy, safety in a situation that is unsafe, control in a situation that is terrifyingly unpredictable, power in a situation of helplessness. These children can become master tacticians, with senses fine-tuned to the onset of violence and danger.

When my friend and co-author Jess Halloran showed me that passage, I felt as though it could have been written about me. My coping strategies were things like compartmentalising, putting on a brave face even when I was going through hell, subconsciously blocking out a lot of bad stuff to protect myself – to this day people tell me about certain things that happened in those days and I can't remember them.

My way to survive was to follow my father's instructions, his rules, without fail. The way he operated was that people were there to be used. Not to be cared for, or relied on, or trusted, or loved. He was almost purely transactional. You can see it in the way he made me sack the coaches I loved, who were good for my game, for my wellbeing and who supported me. He would get rid of people the moment he felt they weren't thinking in the same way he did. He made sure I didn't get too close to them, so I couldn't get comfortable enough to tell them what was really going on in our family.

I am often asked why I didn't say anything, tell anyone – including coaches who I was close to, had respect for, and who wanted the best for me – what he was doing to me over all those years. You know why I lied about the bruises? About all of it? I thought – no, I knew – he would kill me if I told the truth. He would kill me if I even hinted to anyone outside of my family that something was wrong, that I was abused almost daily and was living in constant fear at home.

I had two lives. A private life in which I dealt with my father's cruelty and abuse, and a public one where I maintained a tough veneer that I was fine – all with a stony, sad face.

When you bury abuse and secrets so deep, the abuse becomes normalised, and it's very hard to extricate yourself from that pattern of thinking.

So I am humbled that at every single presentation or motivational talk I've given, survivors of family violence have come up to me and shared their story. I feel humbled that they confide in me, but at the same time it is incredibly scary and sad that this is the reality for too many.

I meet people who are so terrified, living in the middle of a family violence situation. I can see the fear and trauma they are carrying. I see it on their faces. I hear it in their voices. I know what that feels like. And they thank me for sharing my story because it feels to them as though I am speaking for them, like they are heard. They know I understand why they have suffered in silence or are still suffering in silence. They can identify with my story and it resonates with them. It also gives them hope that just maybe there is a light at the end of the tunnel.

Child abuse: 'out of sight and out of mind'

Society's silence around abuse was highlighted by a 2021 report by the Australian Childhood Foundation, which concluded that 'child abuse is still out of sight and out of mind'. The Childhood Foundation's findings in 2021 were similar to those of previous decades, which indicated that 'child abuse is of less concern to the community than problems with public transport and roads. Not only is there a lack of awareness of the issues that children face, but also a lack of belief of children who disclose abuse.'

Dr Joe Tucci and Janise Mitchell of the Childhood Foundation wrote of the shocking numbers of children still suffering at the hands of their parents or carers: 'Approximately, 486,300 reports of child abuse and neglect were made to statutory child protection systems across the country in 2019–20. This resulted in the circumstances of more than 174,000 children and young people being investigated by child protection officers. That equates to 1 investigation every 3 minutes.'

It is clear that today child abuse is still an awful problem. It is horrifying to know how widespread the issue remains throughout our society and that the silence around it is still very real. This silence must end. We *must* keep these children at the front of our minds and work out ways not only to bring them to the public's attention but also to help them.

Scars

The scars us survivors wear are deep. Not only are we likely to suffer devastating effects as a result of abuse, but because of the shame we feel about what we endured, and the behaviours the abuse might have caused, we are likely to stay silent – sometimes for decades, sometimes for our whole lives.

The Australian government's Institute of Health and Welfare describes how

> child abuse and neglect can have a wide range of significant adverse impacts on a child's development and later outcomes, including but not limited to: reduced social skills, poor school performance, impaired language ability, higher likelihood of criminal offending, negative physical health outcomes, mental health issues such as eating disorders, substance abuse, depression and suicide.

Unquestionably I have suffered some of these impacts. I know that victims of emotional abuse also experience feelings of self-hatred, self-destructiveness, self-neglect, rage and feelings of isolation. Again, I have experienced many of those feelings, intensely. If we're talking of feelings of self-hatred, many times in the past I looked to my abuser for healing. My father blamed me for breaking up our family unit, so I reached out to him, desperate to 'fix' the relationship between us. And the reason I did this was not only to show my family I wasn't a traitor, but also because I thought that if I could make things better with my father, I would feel better with myself and in turn my pain and feelings of shame, guilt and self-loathing would go away. I blamed myself. Abusers are manipulators – they avoid responsibility for their actions by throwing the blame back on to those they are harming, and making their victims believe they are the problem. It was only many years later that I realised that victims are *never* to blame.

Speaking up

My previous terror of talking about my abuse, my conditioning to be silent, have changed now I'm an adult who has managed to extricate herself from her abuser. Doing that was extremely difficult, but I know now that something you might consider to be shameful and an embarrassment, something around which there's a stigma, can be destigmatised if it is shared.

Today those of us who can speak up need to keep having more open conversations around domestic violence and child abuse, as well as about mental health. It's not easy at times to turn up and talk about what you have lived but I see it now as my responsibility to help others to use my voice for issues like these. Issues that people still find uncomfortable to talk about and listen to.

Croatian player Mirjana Lucic-Baroni also suffered abuse from her father when she was on the tennis circuit. After *Unbreakable* was published in the US, she told the *New York Times*, 'My heart broke for [Jelena] . . . We are members of this unfortunate club, so to speak. We've never discussed it, but I knew about her and she knew about me. It's a really tough cycle, and it's not something that you're going to talk to somebody about.'

Mirjana is quite right – it's not easy to talk about these problems. Because we are ashamed to. I certainly was – I was embarrassed about what I'd been through, and afraid to talk about it with anyone, and certainly publicly. And yet, towards the end of my tennis career I was slowly gathering courage and considering opening up for the first time because I wanted to try to challenge that silence. It was an extremely frightening idea because of that conditioning to keep things behind closed doors. I started to realise that society was conditioned the same way. It felt shameful to come out and say you've been beaten your whole life.

But I found the courage. I knew that not everyone had a platform, but I did. I felt like when I was young, I had no one to look up to who'd survived abuse. I wanted to break the mould. I felt like my father got away with a lot and that I'd paid the price, over and over. I decided to do away with the shame and stigma and write my story.

I decided to tell my story in 2016 – pre #MeToo. Writing started in October of that year, a time when, as far as I knew, no international sportsperson had detailed their suffering in an abusive relationship in the same way I was about to.

A year later, on 5 October 2017, a month before the publication of *Unbreakable*, journalists Megan Twohey and Jodi Kantor of the *New York Times* broke the story about Hollywood legend Harvey Weinstein's pattern of sexual assaults, harassment and bullying. Ten days after that, actress Alyssa Milano tweeted, 'If you've been sexually harassed or assaulted write "me too" as a reply to this tweet', and the MeToo hashtag went viral.

In the years since, Weinstein has been convicted and jailed as a sexual predator, and many other powerful men have been uncovered as having assaulted women – actors, judges, artists, singers, rappers, all finally being brought to justice after those who had previously been silenced found the courage in the uprising to tell their stories and report the crimes committed against them.

In Australia Grace Tame, alongside activist and journalist Nina Funnell, fought bravely for the right to tell her story of being sexually abused as a student by her teacher. For her advocacy she was awarded the title of Australian of the Year in 2021.

It was extraordinary to watch all these women speaking out, and empowering to hear other victims tell their stories with such bravery. All of them reiterate to me that we need to keep raising our voices. We are stronger in numbers. I alone could change someone's world, but together we can change the world. And this change, in different areas, started because of a few women speaking up.

If we can be open about our pain and experiences, maybe we have a chance to create a world with less pain, more love, support and understanding. Ultimately a better world.

Abuse in sport

The 2017 #MeToo outpouring had its roots in the film industry, but it was happening in sport as well. Also in October 2017, Olympic gymnast McKayla Maroney tweeted that she had been sexually assaulted by former team doctor Larry Nassar, which led to other US gymnasts coming forward with similar allegations. Nassar later pleaded guilty to charges of criminal sexual conduct and federal child pornography charges.

By the time Nassar was sentenced in December 2017, more than 150 women had come forward with horrific testimonies of what he had done to them. I knew exactly why those women and girls had been silent until then. It was because of the fear of blame, shame, stigma and not being believed by society. It was chilling, gut-wrenching and incredibly brave of these women to tell their stories. After hearing some of them speak, in January 2018 the judge sentenced Nassar to up to 175 years in prison for his crimes. The judge said, 'I just signed your death warrant' – Nassar had already been sentenced to sixty years on federal child pornography charges.

That same month superstar gymnast Simone Biles, who'd dominated the Rio 2016 Olympics, where she'd won four gold medals, described the abuse she suffered at the hands of Nassar in a statement posted on Twitter: 'Most of you know me as a happy, giggly, and energetic girl,' she wrote. 'But lately I've felt a bit broken and the more I try to shut off the voice in my head the louder it screams.

'I am not afraid to tell my story anymore. I too am one of the many survivors that was sexually abused by Larry Nassar. Please believe me when I say it was a lot harder to first speak those words out loud than it is now to put them on paper. There are many reasons that I have been reluctant to share my story . . . for too long I've asked myself . . . "Was it my fault?" I now know the answer to those questions. No. No, it was not my fault. No, I will not and should not carry the guilt that belongs to Larry Nassar, USAG, and others.'

The guilt that Biles talks about, I really understand that, and the self-blame you carry as a victim – it can paralyse you in the most debilitating way.

In the 2020s, more scandals centring around abuse in sport were exposed. Abuse was reported in figure skating, athletics and swimming, around the world and in Australia. In the US a report was published in October 2022 about their National Women's Soccer League. The *New York Times* described the report as 'a troubling history of abuse in the sport, from youth leagues to the professional ranks. The voices of powerful female athletes were either cast aside or diminished. Too often they felt they had nowhere to turn. Coaches controlled careers and held nearly unfettered sway.' The *Times* said the behaviour of these coaches was all about power – 'who has it, and who does not . . . Who can't seem to help using it to dehumanize, belittle, abuse, and cross every boundary of decency.' All of this sounded very familiar to me.

In 2022, years after a difficult time in her life, tennis star turned coach and commentator Pam Shriver decided to talk publicly about experiences she'd had as a teenager, speaking to a journalist for the first time about how she'd had a sexual relationship with her coach, former Australian tennis player Don Candy. She explained how she was in a five-year-long 'inappropriate' relationship with Candy, after she'd declared that she was in love with him when she was only seventeen and Candy was fifty.

In the UK *Daily Telegraph* she described the affair as a 'traumatic experience', which Candy should have never allowed to take place as an authority figure who was decades older than she was. She called for an end to the toxic culture of sexual relationships between female players and their coaches.

'The way forward has to lie in a new system of credentialing which applies to anyone in a support team – whether it's a coach, a physio or a fitness trainer,' Shriver wrote. 'Anti-abuse should be as important as anti-doping and anti-match-fixing, and the rules as clearly laid down.'

She had the same attitude as I do when it comes to trying to stop abuse in tennis and sport in general, saying, 'I'm making this story public because I hope it will make a difference.'

I followed the stories as they unfolded around the world, and they reinforced to me that one of the ways to change these cultures is to keep challenging our inclination to silence. The whole issue of abuse needs to come out of the dark places of sport.

But are the authorities ready to listen? Often the road-blocks to action are the power structures. For example, for too many years there has not been a way of reporting abuse in sports independently. The practice of calling out poor or toxic behaviour has been left to victims.

In September 2022 former tennis world No. 1 Victoria Azarenka said that the WTA needs to do more to protect young players from abuse by coaches and people in positions of power in tennis. She alleged that abuse happens 'left and right on the Tour', and called on the association to improve safeguards for players.

A few months later, in January 2023, in an interview with *The Age*, Pam also asked if the WTA was doing enough in terms of protection and reporting. 'I don't know if they [WTA] are all in yet,' she told the newspaper.

What the WTA has done is create a position called 'director of safeguarding'. I hope this will help in some way. Like Pam is pushing for, the more people we have around to help players and coaches maintain professional boundaries on the tour, the better. Because there are an incredible number of young women on the tour. That was the case when I was playing and remains so now. There are many, many young women completely dependent on their coach and it's important there are mechanisms in place to ensure these women are safe.

As I wrote in *Unbreakable* in 2017:

I know I was not the only one suffering on the tour . . . the tour can be a very difficult and lonely place for women, especially because most of us start to play professionally at a young age; fifteen, sixteen. You are very vulnerable. Most players travel without their parents, especially when they are starting out, because of lack of finances. They just take a coach for their tennis. That's why female tennis players should have support and protection.

It's the same when it comes to abusive parents on the tour because it's an extremely complex situation – and it's more common than people realise; it starts at a very young age, especially for girls, and at the grassroots level. More than ten years ago, University of Miami tennis coach Mario Rincon told the *Miami Herald*, 'Tennis parents can really get out of control, and, unfortunately, we see it all the time. It's the ugly part of our sport nobody likes to talk about. Something should be done. Over the years, we have come across many really good players with crazy parents . . . It's so sad.' This is still true today.

Now, I don't know whether the WTA's safeguarding position would have had any effect on my life if it had existed back when I was playing. But it's a start.

And the WTA is not alone in trying to make things better. Tennis Australia has also tried to address the issue of abuse on the tour, with a 2022 policy called 'A Safer Game Plan', to educate tennis club officials about the potential for abuse between coaches and players. It also encourages young players to speak up if they're feeling unsafe.

But of course, that is easier said than done when the abuser is the one who's making very sure you won't speak. So I really hope that all of this helps, and importantly, let's continue making a safe space and environment for victims and survivors to feel comfortable to speak up, so we can create change.

My mission

- It's so important to encourage people, women, especially young girls to know their voice matters.
- I want to be able to use my platform and my experience to empower people, women and the younger generation so that they know they deserve the world, that abuse is not okay, that they have a voice.
- I would like us to use our voices to create a safe space and united community. Silence is the abuser's power, control, manipulation and it creates fear.
- It's time to listen to survivors' stories, for us as a society and to change the world for future generations. They deserve better.

- Speaking up shows survivors that they are not alone. It helps raise awareness and it shows how widespread and global abuse is.
- We need to address this issue at the grassroots. Young girls and boys need to know abusive behaviour is not okay and can be reported safely.
- When we share, we heal, we free ourselves and we connect both as individuals and as a united community. We are stronger in numbers.
- I now truly believe in the saying 'If you can see it, you can be it; if you can hear it, you can say it.'

Mantra: In silence darkness thrives. I use my voice to inspire others and call out injustice, in the hope of making a difference and creating change.

2.

BODY

Size shouldn't matter. Kindness and being a
good person matter.

Over the past five years, I have been nothing but honest about the majority of my mental health battles. But my disordered eating is something I haven't been able to face addressing or delving deeply into until now. Why? Because I didn't understand it. I didn't even know this was what I was going through. I want to share it with you now because I think the more we talk about the issues around our bodies and perceptions of them, and around body-shaming in our society, the more these issues become destigmatised and hopefully start to be fixed.

I think it was a great move making Taryn Brumfitt the 2023 Australian of the Year. I loved her words when she accepted the honour: 'We weren't born into the world hating our bodies.

This is something society has taught us. Body-shaming is a universal problem.'

But as Taryn says, when it comes to this issue, so much work needs to be done. Especially as it affects children. 'It's getting younger and younger,' Taryn observed. 'I spoke to a six-year-old recently who was dieting. We really need to help our kids across Australia and the world because the rates of suicide, eating disorders, anxiety, depression, steroid use, are all on the increase, related to body dissatisfaction.'

So I'd like to share with you my experiences and issues of body, weight, dieting and how they all relate to mental health. Here goes.

Hunger

I first felt the ravenous ache of hunger when I was eight years old.

In June 1991, as war erupted in Yugoslavia, my mother, three-month-old baby brother Savo and I fled to Serbia to escape the fighting. My father stayed back home in Osijek, Croatia. As refugees we found ourselves living in a small storage shed in a city called Sombor. We had limited water, limited electricity, limited heating in winter; there was an old double bed, a bassinet for Savo, and from the moment we arrived there was a scarcity of food. One of my overwhelming memories of that time is feeling hungry. Food was hard to come by because of a lack of money and the war, which affected the supply of staples like bread and milk. One source was from the Red Cross, who'd give us a small cardboard box of basics, including flour. I remember my mother baking bread for us – mixing the dough up in the evening, covering it with a warm cloth and leaving it on a high shelf in the warmest corner of the room. Inevitably, disgustingly, rats or mice would find their way into the sticky dough. They would be wrenched out by Mum and the dough would have to be thrown away. It's a grotesque memory I find hard to erase to this day. Unsurprisingly, I have a fierce fear of rodents.

When the dough remained rat-free and my mum could bake it, I'd eat her bread ravenously but always hoping for more. We had a lot of days where we went hungry. Chocolate was like a far-off dream.

As a refugee I was enrolled in a local primary school and soon found my way to a tennis court and club. I incessantly and obsessively practised – and with little food I was skinny. I was accepting of this way of life, though there were plenty of times that I went to bed hungry.

The lack of food, especially of much wholesome food, didn't go away even when we arrived in Australia – again as refugees – in 1994, this time with my father in tow. Our first home in this new country was a tiny apartment in Fairfield, Sydney, in which all four of us would twist ourselves onto a double bed mattress to sleep.

Soon my mother found work in Fairfield's Tip Top bread factory. One of the things we'd eat was leftover bread she brought home, spread with margarine (because it was cheaper than butter) and table salt.

It was around this time, 1994, that the pressure and abuse in my young life got even worse. That pressure and abuse, of course, came from my father. I vividly remember waking most mornings in absolute panic and worry. How can I make sure he doesn't hurt me today? How can I make sure he doesn't explode? The violence and the outbursts from him were escalating. His drinking quickly got out of hand in Australia. As soon as we moved here he began spiralling out of control when it came to alcohol. He was by then drinking heavily at my junior tournaments.

After losses in matches, 'bad' matches in his eyes, and after long practice sessions during which I trained my heart out, absolutely flogging myself, he would punish me by making me run home along the Hume Highway, a distance of 10 kilometres, even in the intense heat of the Sydney summer.

While he dictated my diet, insisted I was lean for athletic purposes, he also denied me food if he thought I had trained terribly. In other words, he weaponised food. Starving me was a punishment. Denying me water was a punishment. But, like everything on his watch, it was enforced to a dangerous degree, not being able to hydrate and eat 'well' were taken to horrible, extreme levels.

After these torture sessions, when I would train hard and then be denied food, my grandmother – who was living with us at that time – would sometimes in the middle of the night come into my room to secretly give me something to eat. I vividly remember her slipping quietly in to deliver me Tip Top plain white toast with a little bit of Nutella on it – while my father was sleeping, of course.

As for 'treats'? When my father did allow me a treat, I literally had to make it last for weeks. There was a WTA tournament in Amelia Island, South Carolina, that sums up how food and 'treats' were dealt with under his authority. My father and I found a beautiful little store that sold many different types of Oreos. You could buy them by the biscuit. We walked into this incredible shop and there were Oreos covered in white chocolate, in milk chocolate and in dark chocolate. And my father allowed me to take one of each. Which was a surprise, because he rarely rewarded me for anything I achieved on the court. I cradled three of them in a small bag. But I wasn't able to eat them straight away. He wouldn't let me. He was like, 'Okay. These have to last for a couple of weeks.' Of course, I made sure they did.

Another intense episode of being denied food came later on in my tennis career, at the 2000 du Maurier Open in Montreal. I lost a very close first-round match to Belgium's Sabine Appelmans. That night my father psychologically destroyed me, calling me names and kicking me with his sharp dress shoes. He knocked me unconscious and on top of that denied me food from the end of the match until the following evening. It absolutely broke me, physically and mentally. Bruises marked my skin for weeks after, and my soul forever.

Bingeing

I can't pinpoint exactly when I started to binge on food but the compulsions began after I'd escaped my abusive situation – I left my family and ran away from the terrible world my father had created for me.

Despite the hell I was leaving, I was heartbroken to go. I was at a tennis tournament in Russia when I decided that I would leave my family unit. It was just my mother and me in Russia on this part of the tennis tour. And so, on a cool Moscow night in early October 2002, I slipped a 'goodbye' letter under her hotel door. In that letter, which I wrote with tears streaming down my cheeks, I asked her for forgiveness and told her this was simply something I had to do.

On the plane, as I fled, an intense wave of sadness washed over me. As soon as I left I started feeling incredibly low. And with this scary feeling of misery, slowly food became an issue for me. The anxiety and sadness and confusion I was feeling around that time began to manifest in some weird ways, which were completely new to me. I was someone who'd never really thought about food. Now, I was starting to think about it all the time. I would do things like buying a Kit-Kat and eating only the chocolate coating. It wasn't that I didn't like the wafer. In my mind I was balancing eating for comfort while convincing myself that I wasn't overdoing it. What I didn't realise was that this was the beginning of disordered eating habits.

Until then, I had been a person who didn't really crave sweets and desserts – I knew they weren't available to me, and I had a lot else to worry about. Remember, I could make three Oreos last weeks. I didn't live for food, I wasn't obsessed by it, I didn't pay that much attention to it. I didn't care about it really.

Before October 2002, because of my father's brutal fitness regimen, his punishments of starving me for short periods, his control of my food intake, one thing I'd never had to worry about was my physical fitness or weight. But as the months and years rolled on through the early 2000s, gradually they became an issue.

Trauma piling on trauma contributed to me craving more and more to eat. Eating began to take over my life. I was turning to food more and more to help me ease my pain. What had been some unusual habits which were fairly benign turned into some more problematic behaviours. Eating was the first thing I thought of when I woke, and on certain days, as the hours unfolded, I'd constantly seek out food until I went to bed again. This turned into bingeing. Eating made me feel good. For me, it was comforting to binge. In some eating disorders, you feel like food is not going to let you down. I know now from the experts in my life that depression and over-eating are strongly linked. I was using food as a coping mechanism as symptoms of depression arose. Food would take away emotional pain in the moment. It was basically my trauma response.

Australia's Butterfly Foundation, which supports those suffering eating disorders, say that research shows that people like me are prime candidates to end up suffering complex relationships with food: 'We know that discrimination, trauma, and exposure to violence and abuse can increase someone's risk of developing a body image issue or eating disorder. In addition, pressure to conform to social or cultural stereotypes can also play a part.'

The bingeing grew from craving sweets to fixating on carbs – stuff like pizza, large amounts of pasta. But sugar was my biggest weakness. I would buy an entire cake and eat four to five slices at a time. Before, I hadn't much cared for cake – until all of a sudden I was someone who would eat multiple helpings one after the other. I would sometimes binge bags of chocolate before playing. All this spiked my sugar levels to no end and made me feel awful on court. But then I'd feel an enormous amount of guilt, so I would try to fix it by starving myself for a day. When I say starving, I mean that after six hours of training I would reward myself with a tomato. A solitary tomato is all I would allow myself to eat. I had to undo the sins of the day before and this was the only way I knew how to. Bingeing/starving. I also turned to laxatives, as well as sometimes punishing myself for hours on the treadmill.

It was an erratic schedule. I would binge one day and fast the next. Some days I would binge for three days and then starve myself for the next three. It was all dependent on my emotional state. It was dependent on my anxiety and my depression levels. I would sometimes be 'good' for a week, and then fall into bingeing. From the outside you wouldn't have known anything was wrong because even though I binged, I could control the weight by training hard and playing a lot of tennis. But there came a point where the amount I was eating meant it was not possible to control my weight.

I now understand that this bingeing was closely connected to the heightened state of anxiety, depression and trauma I was living with.

Around these years, I knew that I was starting behind everyone else on tour when it came to being physically well prepared for my matches. My disordered eating was also affecting me mentally because I was thinking more about food than about my tennis and my life in general. Quite simply, you feel awful when you binge and you feel awful when you starve, and those feelings are all-consuming. I wasn't thinking about anything else except self-loathing, or what I would eat next.

I was deeply uncomfortable in the locker room as my weight fluctuated. I felt so much shame. I felt alone. I was desperately trying to get the starving and bingeing cycle under control, but I couldn't. At the time I was sure I was the only person on tour living in this awful cycle, that no other player had this type of relationship with food. You feel like a failure because you can't break the cycle. I hated myself because I couldn't get myself back to 'normal'. That is, eating without a care and for fuel rather than because of emotions. I hated my body. Absolutely detested it. Other women seemed so confident heading out to the court and in training. They seemed to be comfortable in their own skin where I felt nothing but discomfort.

I didn't know of anyone else on the tour with an eating disorder. It was a highly competitive, ruthless environment,

and it wasn't a place to talk about 'feelings' or show any vul-
nerabilities. I didn't feel there was anyone I could talk to about
this. I was actually completely unaware that I was well in the
throes of a full-blown eating disorder. And I was getting some
bad advice from people around me. One of my coaches would
constantly tell me to 'cut carbs', and insisted I eat just a can
of tuna with lemon juice as a meal. This person was obsessed
with women being thin and would literally count every bite
I was taking at meals. You really should not say these things
to anyone, let alone to an athlete training hard, and for me it
made everything ten times worse.

In December 2005, as I tried to re-establish my once rocket-
ing tennis career, the press was again focusing on me – and
not for my tennis. They were being unkind about the shape
I was in. 'Jelena Dokic is about to spend her first Christmas
in Melbourne,' wrote one sportswriter. 'She would be wise to
avoid the plum pudding as she inches back towards peak competitive shape.' For the record, at this time I weighed only three
kilograms more than I had when I was in my best competitive
shape.

I remember reading those words and feeling absolutely
flattened. I mean, that observation is extremely cruel, not to
mention unjustified. Looking back, however, I don't know
why I was surprised. There has always been body-shaming in
sport, and certainly in society more generally, and throughout
the media. Remember a time when women's magazines were
emblazoned with pictures of so-and-so celebrity in a bikini
with a headline referring to 'a few extra kilos'? And in the

years since, when I have been repeatedly humiliated by horrible comments such as the one in December 2005, awful stories have emerged from figure skaters, runners and swimmers – almost always women – who were body-shamed through their careers by coaches and others in power around them.

It's only now that women are finding their voices to speak candidly about what they went through as athletes. And believe me, there are still lots of women who don't talk about it, and are afraid to. Olympic champion Libby Trickett was one of the first Australian swimmers to speak out about the issues she's had with her body, going from a multi-gold medallist to a mother. Now she's a mum of four, Libby has spoken often about body positivity. I was fortunate enough to be a guest on her 'All That Glitters' podcast, where I discussed my story. She is a great ally to women. When Broncos star Julia Robinson was body-shamed for showcasing her body, which was described as 'too masculine' for a woman, Libby was right there backing her. Libby posted a picture of herself that showed the strength that saw her become a triple Olympic champion. 'Muscles are cool,' she wrote.

They show how hard you've worked to hone your vehicle to do the thing that you've been training it to do.

Women, and in this case female athletes, get a huge amount of scrutiny about their bodies through social media, mainstream media and societal expectations. Screw that. Muscles are cool, chubby is beautiful, different abilities are remarkable.

In early 2023, I was fortunate to be publicly supported by a great many people when I called out those trolling me, body-shaming me, and one of those supporters was Taryn Brumfitt. In an interview with Channel 10's *The Project*, Taryn made the point strongly that the bullying I faced was not okay. 'Bullying is never okay and I think we need to call it out. I think we are getting better in this country at doing that,' she said. 'I know how it feels to be trolled and how it feels to have those naysayers but if we keep leading with light and love there's nothing more powerful than that.'

But while there are great voices like those of Taryn and Libby, it remains a small minority who are willing to go there. I get it. It is hard for so many people. Which is why I continue to raise my voice today.

I want this to become a natural, open discussion around body image so we can blitz the shame associated with the issue.

Peaks and troughs

Eventually, at the end of 2008, I got back to almost my peak form. Something switched where I found my drive to train again. I worked hard to have balance in my life – eating well, training well. Sometimes I could control my eating disorder for six months at a stretch. So by the time the Australian summer came around at the start of 2009 I was ready to fight on the court again.

I was ranked 187 when I won a wild card into the 2009 Australian Open. From there an amazing sporting chapter of my life unfolded. In the first round I brought down Austrian player Tamira Paszek in three sets. It was an incredible victory and my first at a grand slam since 2003.

Next, I did away with No. 17 Anna Chakvetadze in a second-round three-setter. Then I claimed Caroline Wozniacki (11th seed), and Alisa Kleybanova (29th seed). I smashed my way through these three-set matches. After them I was spent but the momentum, and winning again, galvanised me. I still had my fight.

I made the quarter-finals to face the No. 3 seed, Russia's Dinara Safina. But all good things must come to an end. Safina was able to beat me on the day – she was third seed for a reason.

My ranking had reached No. 56 by the end of 2009, but my tennis would never hit the heights it once had, because of a shoulder injury, wrist injury and glandular fever, which hit me hard in 2009 and 2010. I've never quite recovered from the fatigue caused by glandular fever. My disordered eating wrecked my body and my mind. I was broken, had nothing left and was forced to retire.

As my career started to unwind, and then I retired, I really started to struggle mentally with my purpose in life, and my eating disorder started to escalate.

The world I was living in, where your body is on show most days due to the outfits we wear, combined with my background of enduring years of abuse, set me up to suffer like I did and have. With the pain of my childhood and youth unresolved,

I was living with a lot of emotional pain. Over the years of 2010, 2011 and 2012, I returned to the cycle of bingeing and starving.

By early 2017 I weighed 120 kilograms, almost twice the weight I'd been when I played. The shame returned, and I didn't have the skills to cope with my emotions around it all. I found myself emotionally eating again and when I embarked on the book-writing process I was not feeling that well. The shame I felt was so immense, it really affected my everyday existence. It robbed me of some amazing experiences and opportunities. Eventually I became afraid to leave the house; I turned down work opportunities because of my insecurity around my size.

Brené Brown defines shame as 'an intensely painful feeling or experience that we are flawed and therefore unworthy of love and belonging'. Shame makes life awful.

Understanding and addressing eating and emotions

As you can see, eating is something I have trouble controlling. It's emotional eating. I'm very aware of that now, but I haven't been until recently. Now I am working hard to heal, and I hope not to ever bear so much shame around my weight again. I'm at a place where I feel comfortable in my own body, no matter what size I am. As I write this book, my body image is something that for the first time in my life I am working through from a psychological perspective. I mean, there was a point where I knew, you know, there was something going on when it came to my eating and my emotions – that there were triggers and certain reasons for my spiralling at certain times, but I never properly understood it until recently.

All these episodes from my childhood and youth, I really hadn't made the connection to my disordered eating until a session with a psychiatrist in March 2022. It might seem crazy to you that it took me so long to make those links, but it is what living with trauma does to you. When you are in the thick of it, you lurch from one moment to the next, just reacting. All that reaction means there's little left in your brain to try to analyse how you've got to where you are.

It really didn't occur to me that my cravings, my bingeing, were in part due to what had happened to me in my formative years until the psychiatrist pointed out a couple of fundamental truths.

One: I had grown up worrying where my next meal would be coming from and if I would be full enough after eating it. Two: I am still suffering the trauma of having lived in a highly abusive family environment for more than two decades.

At a session in July 2022 the psychiatrist connected the dots for me. He explained that food makes me feel good, it lifts my mind out of the darkness. I use it to control my feelings in a short-term way: eating makes me feel better for a bit, until the shame and sadness of over-eating kicks in. Eating gives me comfort and doesn't disappoint like so many other things in my life did. I found comfort and safety in food.

Since then I have read that 90 per cent of disordered eating happens because of traumatic events.

The facts on binge eating

According to the Inside Out Institute for Eating Disorders, 'a Binge Eating Disorder (BED) is a type of eating disorder characterised by recurrent episodes of binge eating. A binge is defined as eating an amount of food that is larger than what most people would eat in a similar period of time. While eating, the person has a sense of lack of control.'

The institute observes that bingeing episodes often are a result of sufferers responding to emotional difficulties instead of hunger. They can be a way of coping with issues such as boredom, loneliness and anxiety, to numb or distract from these problems. Or eating in this disordered way can be because of anxieties about food itself, connected to concerns about your weight or perceived body shape.

Almost always, points out the institute, binges are followed by feelings of guilt, shame, disgust and depression.

Inside Out estimates that one million Australians are living with an eating disorder – that is 4 per cent of the population.

Raising my voice

My weight is not only my own private issue, as I've found since establishing my TV and commentary career, and having a public profile.

From a young age, I became accustomed to living a public life. Of course, being in the public eye was awful at times – when my father was losing his mind throughout my greatest tennis years and causing me all sorts of grief.

Years on from that, some of the scrutiny has focused instead on my weight. I have seen people look at me differently as it has fluctuated. I have seen the look in their eyes when I'm a smaller size. I've felt people embrace me more when I've lost large amounts of weight. At times I have been treated with respect and celebrated for it.

At one stage, a few years ago, I was able to lose quite a bit of weight. It took an enormous amount of work: I intensely watched what I ate, I found a love for exercise again. The smaller I became, the more I saw that look on people's faces of 'your body – and therefore you – are more acceptable now'. People admired my ability to transform myself physically. The platitudes came my way.

But in the end I put a lot of that weight back on because what I hadn't yet dealt with were the psychological and emotional aspects of bingeing and starving cycles.

What do those cycles look like?

I would sometimes eat literally ten times a day. I would eat the amount of food and calories you would usually eat in four or five days. I would have two breakfasts, two lunches, two dinners, consisting of things like five slices of cake, three burgers, two servings of fries, bars of chocolate, sandwiches for snacks.

But then I had the ability to starve myself.

I could go for six days without food – that was my record, and I would be training as well. By training, I mean playing at least five hours of tennis a day. Outside my tennis career I would do the same but instead of on-court training, I'd be going to the gym and running a lot. I would feel sick from too much food, and then I would feel unwell and dizzy from not enough food. I never felt good.

Overcoming hate

Because at that point, I wasn't dealing with the root causes of my disordered eating, the cycles would repeat again and again.

And with that came the 'looks' and nastiness. I have had direct messages on Instagram accusing me of being 'too fat', 'unrecognisable'. People would call me names like 'whale' and 'pig' on social media, and I'd overhear horrible comments, stuff like 'What happened to her?' One person even said that no matter how good a commentator I was, he couldn't listen to me knowing I was fat.

Of course, these messages and remarks make me feel terrible.

And, as I touched on earlier, I am not alone. Despite great work being done in this area by brave and brilliant women like Taryn, we live in a body-shaming culture. What I have learnt from speaking about my weight is that many people go through what I have gone through. So many people have told me that their weight gain, like mine, comes from a painful place. They have also struggled and tried relentlessly to reduce their weight. It's extremely hard. I know this so well. It's a battle. I consider it a privilege that people are willing to confide in me and it's a lot because I see their suffering too.

Studies have shown an unmistakeable connection between eating disorders and childhood trauma, but of course plenty of people who have a difficult relationship with food, whose body shape is larger than others, haven't necessarily been through trauma or used food as a coping mechanism in the way I did. Either way, being body-shamed is a terrible experience and is never okay.

I won't always let the hateful comments on social media slide. Early in both 2021 and 2022 were two occasions when I'd had enough and decided to respond to the latest slinging I was getting in my DMs and publicly. In February 2021 I wrote a post calling out these anonymous keyboard warriors. With this post I wanted to remind people that they never know which battle someone is fighting behind closed doors. And so, for the first time I stood up to those who had negatively referred to my size.

Dokic_Jelena ✅

I have always been honest with you all about my struggles and my weight battles. I have talked about my weight and not a lot of people have done that publicly.

Now I am also going to be honest but I also feel like I need to address the negative attention around what people think I should look like. And here is my message to you, get over it. Leave me and my physical appearance alone.

I really don't know why people have the need to comment on someone's physical appearance, especially when it comes to women.

You would never talk like that about a man,
it's always about women and their appearance.
While I am nowhere near my heaviest, I am also
completely honest about the fact that I have put
some weight back on in the Melbourne lockdown.

It was very hard mentally for me in the world's
toughest lockdown for six months and not being
able to see my loved ones for 15 months.

If you have nothing nice to say, don't say
anything at all.

How about a bit of kindness? How about a
message asking me how I am doing? Instead
of talking about my weight, why don't you talk
about all my accomplishments? Does my weight
determine my worth?

It's so easy to judge others but why can't people
just be kind? We should be talking about inner
beauty and not the shallow outside looks.

But the trolling didn't stop. A year later I was pushed again to respond. And why were people coming back at me at that particular time? I was back on their television screens. Like clockwork the comments came as a result of me being on TV during the Australian Open.

Sure, stuff like this comes with being in the public eye. People feel like they can criticise you and judge you and make comments about you and your views. And they can, that's true. But that doesn't make the slurs and venom all right.

So when those messages flooded in referencing my weight gain, I opened up my phone and I poured out my heart on Instagram:

Dokic_Jelena ✅

I can't believe I have to address this again!

I am being body shamed again and I am seeing comments and even articles about my weight and appearance. It's disgusting behaviour.

JUST STOP ALREADY. NOT JUST WHEN IT COMES TO ME BUT OTHER PEOPLE AS WELL, ESPECIALLY WOMEN.

This is a serious problem and one that women face all the time.

I have said it before and I will say it again, STOP COMMENTING ON MY WEIGHT AND SIZE.

It is not kind and it's ignorant.

I am strong, I can take it and I don't care about you but I will call it out. By doing this you might be doing damage and hurting someone else out there that you know nothing about and you have no idea what they might be going through.

Stop judging me based on my size.

You shouldn't be judging me at all.

Is my worth and if I am a good person really determined by my size?

I get comments like, why are you so fat?

Or, you are unrecognisable? And my favourite is, what happened to you?

Well a shit load has happened but I am here and I am fighting but that's not what you care about. You only care about my weight and how to make fun of it.

I am also seeing images that are photoshopped to make me look bigger and you can clearly see how my head is so disproportionate to my body.

It's disgusting and those who have done it should be ashamed of themselves and so should those that are writing articles about my weight.

Would you do the same if it was your sister, mother or daughter in that position and how would you feel about them being body shamed?

Think about that for a second.

I have never hid the fact that I struggle with my weight. NEVER. It's been a battle for me for a while especially since battling depression.

But I am not ashamed of my size.

I will continue to work on myself but not for the sake of looking better but feeling better and being healthier.

Oh and here is a picture and video of me from today and it's not photoshopped like what some of you have done to make me look bigger.

As always to the 99 percent of you that support me so much, thank you.

It means the world to me and I love you all.

Be kind.

I feel sometimes that no matter how hard I work, no matter how good I am at my job, for the trolls my size is the measure of how good I am – not even just at my job but also as a person. And the fact I am size 16 automatically disqualifies me from being a success in either context, in their eyes.

Sure, I can choose to block or disable comments, but I shouldn't have to block people – I'm not here hurting anyone, so I shouldn't have to be the one to hide from the abuse and bullying. Instead, I will call it out and stand up for what is right – and for others.

In January 2023, the same thing happened *again*. And this time even worse. Of course I wasn't going to take it without addressing it – and making a stand. I addressed it on Instagram during the first week of the Australian Open.

Dokic_Jelena ✔

THE 'BODY SHAMING' AND 'FAT SHAMING' OVER THE LAST 24 HOURS HAS BEEN INSANE.

COMING FROM EVERYWHERE IN THE WORLD AND A SPECIAL SHOUT TO SO MUCH OF IT COMING FROM SERBIA.

AND YES A LOT OF THEM ARE WOMEN TOO.

SO MUCH FOR 'WOMEN SUPPORTING WOMEN'.

Disgusting. People should be so ashamed.

The most common comment being 'what
happened to her, she is so big'?

I will tell you what happened, I am finding a way
and surviving and fighting.

And it really doesn't matter what I am doing and
what happened because size shouldn't matter.
Kindness and being a good person matters which
those of you that abuse me and others, are
clearly not.

What matters is your online abuse, bullying and
fat shaming.

That's what matters because those of you that
do it are just evil, bad, mean and ignorant
people.

I can and will get in shape for myself and my
health but you will not become a better person.

Weight will change but evil people will remain
evil.

I am here, fighting for all those out there being
abused, fat shamed . . .

I can't change the world but I am going to
continue speaking up, calling this behaviour
out, using my platform for something good and

to support other people out there and to give others a voice and try to make others feel less alone and scared.

For all those out there supporting me and there are so many of you, THANK YOU FROM THE BOTTOM OF MY HEART.

And to all of those out there that are genuinely good people, THANK YOU.

I will also be kind and the bigger person unlike you trolls and not reveal your identity.

Love you all, even the trolls because you give me so much motivation and inspiration to do what I do and to fight against people like you.

Love you all xx

Jelena

This post received a lot of media attention, with people from all walks of life, commentators and public figures coming out in support. It made me incredibly emotional to see their supportive articles and messages, and this time round I could feel something was shifting. This was now the third year, during the summer, that I had called out body-shaming and people were starting to listen, especially the media. I was glad to see that the more I stood up to the bullies and social media abuse, the fewer the horrible comments. I was even given the opportunity by Nine to write a piece in their newspapers where I talked more about this problem. We titled the article,

'It's time to declare game, set and match against online trolls'.

Body talk

I understand that many of us don't want to talk about the extra weight we carry. For a very long time I didn't want to talk about it. A mix of reasons motivated me to open up. One was that I have celebrated my fitness 'victories' publicly, so I think it would be wrong not to share when I have faltered. It would be wrong not to share when I've fallen off a 'diet'. It must have happened to every single woman or man who's ever started one. Most diets are highly restrictive and hard to stick to for more than a limited amount of time. Sure, with willpower of steel you can make them work for a certain duration, and lose the kilos. But our bodies are not good at keeping weight off. Diets wreck our metabolism.

My ultimate goal now, in the coming years, is to be the best version of myself. I want to be fit, strong, healthy, but I am not chasing a clothes size or kilos on scales. It doesn't matter if you are a size zero or an 18. It matters what sort of person you are. What you stand for.

I remind myself all the time that our bodies will take many shapes and sizes at different stages of our life, but it is not the size of our body that matters most. It is the size of our character, heart and kindness.

I'm not aiming for a goal weight as I once did. I'm aiming to get fit so that I can also be physically healthy and be able to do other things in life that actually make me happy. I had to remind people of this in April 2023, when I posted two photos on Instagram: one was me as a young woman on court, the other a picture of me commentating now.

Dokic_Jelena ✅

Real, raw, open and honest conversation!

What is the most common comment I see when it comes to my body, size and weight?

What happened to her? I can barely recognise her.

Really? What happened? You can't recognise me?

Let me tell you what happened.

I survived being a refugee twice, I was bullied, I lived in a domestic violence filled home for 15 years and I was beaten unconscious, I was abused physically and emotionally and got beaten for the first time when I was 6 years old. I had to escape home, I battled anxiety, depression, PTSD and trauma and I almost committed suicide.

I still managed to do pretty well, I managed to be top 5 in the world as tennis player and a grand slam finalist, I am a bestselling author, commentator and speaker but most importantly I survived.

So while you see a weight and size change, I will tell you the difference between these two images.

The one on the left is a size 4, scared to death,
beaten unconscious and that bulge on my shins is
from being kicked all night.

The one on the right is me at size 16, I have survived
it all and I am here healing from my trauma and
thriving.

I think the face in the two images says it all.

I will take the size 16 over the size 4 any day if it
means I am happy.

If it means I turned to food to try and survive,
then so be it.

But I am here, I am happy and most importantly
I made it through.

So there is the answer, once and for all.

I went through hell and back and I survived and
today I try to help others.

That's what happened.

And for those that still don't get the point, well
that says everything about you.

Beauty isn't about being a certain size, beauty is
having a beautiful heart and soul.

The way I look as a size 16 has nothing to do with my character or my IQ.

I've been all different sizes. I have been a super-fit athlete and I have also been bigger – but I am grateful for my body in both periods. I've learnt many, many things about myself as a person at all different sizes. While I was playing, I was my fittest and strongest ever, it gave me the possibility to be at the top of my sport. Being a size 16 for the majority of my thirties, well, that's the scars of my trauma in a way, but I am still grateful for it because it was my way of dealing with that trauma and whatever life was throwing at me, and in the end it meant that, with professional help, I learnt more about how to heal.

I'm proud to be a role model and someone who women can identify with in this space – because most women's bodies, be it because of childbirth, hard times, good times, athletic times, will always change. I want to show people that you can accept and appreciate your body, no matter what size.

If you are going through a hard time with your size, it's important not to lose your confidence.

Know this: it is never anyone's business or responsibility to judge your body.

I know it's easy to say this, but try not to take ignorant comments to heart. Try to remember that those comments say more about the person speaking them than they do about you. None of us should be judged for our size. Our legacies should not be about what we look like. Never let anyone put you down or question your worth, especially on your weight. The size of your heart matters, not your body.

Mantra: Your worth is not defined by your size. You are not defined by your size. How you treat others is what defines you.

3.

MENTAL HEALTH

*There is strength within you even when you feel
weak. Keep fighting.*

In May 2022, I was struggling with my mental health. I decided
to write a short letter to myself to try to help me restore my
self-worth. I still have it on my fridge:

You got this, you can do this, so don't give up,
especially on yourself.

Just know you are strong, courageous and
a fighter.

You are getting up and showing up every
single day, no matter how hard things
are. You are trying and doing it over and
over again, no matter what life throws at
you.

Life has thrown a lot at you but you are still here fighting.

Despite all the struggles and inner battles that you are fighting, you still wake up with hope.

You are fighting and not giving up, even though you feel weak and even though it feels like there is nothing left to fight for.

You are in pain, you are hurting, but you still continue to try to heal, and you are a survivor.

There is something incredibly inspiring and powerful in the fact that you continue to believe there is a light at the end of the tunnel even though you can't see it a lot of the time, and that you are holding on to hope even through the darkest times.

So just know you are strong, brave and you got this. You are unbreakable.

Don't give up on yourself. Never.

For me that letter is everything. That is who I am trying to be.

I am trying to show up, not to run from my struggle. I am turning towards the truth and looking it in the eye, and sharing it in turn.

The past

As you know, the darkness had swamped my life well before 2022. The darkness had always been there, disturbing my thoughts, messing with my happiness. These bad feelings plagued me in my playing days and came into full force for the first time when I found myself standing on a balcony in Monaco in 2005. There, I had my first experience of almost taking my own life. I remember the wind howling and whipping my face but on the inside feeling nothing. I was numb. My soul was at rock bottom. My spirit? Almost dead. So I stood on that balcony, thirty storeys up, and I thought about ending it all.

It was three years since I'd left my family unit to escape my abusive father, and I felt like I had abandoned my little brother, Savo. I questioned myself every day about my decision to leave, and to leave him behind. But I had no choice – he was only eleven years old. My father didn't allow him to have any contact with me for years and it broke my heart that I couldn't even talk to him, hear his voice. I blamed myself for it all.

On that day in 2005 I imagined falling, and I did not feel a single ounce of fear about it. I recall putting my hand on the railing and thinking, death is the right thing, there will be peace. If I die, all the grief I feel I am causing will disappear. I thought, everyone else will have peace as well because I am the problem and I will be gone. I wanted my pain to be over.

The suicidal ideation occurred as my passion for tennis was disappearing. I was sleeping for eighteen hours at a time. When I was awake I was barely talking to Tin. And my pain caused me to do the wildly unthinkable to an outsider – or to a person who doesn't know how abuse works: it made me reach out to my father.

Back then, I wanted to fix my relationship with my family. I desperately wanted a civil and loving bond with my parents. With all my heart, I wanted to bring my shattered family back together, and I hoped that my father had changed. I remember saying to Tin, 'I need to figure this out. I want to see if I can work something out,' and I told him I was going to go and see my father in Serbia.

Tin was absolutely perplexed. He knew first-hand the chaos and hell that my father had inflicted on my life. He too had felt the madness. My father had verbally threatened to kill him several times. Tin was scared for my safety. But I was determined to make it all right with my parents, and I thought that by trying to mend this bridge I'd broken by leaving, I could help heal myself and erase the dark thoughts swirling in me daily.

So, I headed back to my father, who was then living in Vrdnik, 70 kilometres outside Belgrade, Serbia, in a palatial home, complete with a tennis court, a gym, a sauna, billiard room, three garages, a 40-metre wine cellar, stables and an orchard so he could make port.

Where did he get the money for this?

The property came from the earnings of my tennis career. Several years earlier I had signed them all over to him in the hope that he would give me some peace. It didn't work. And now, in desperate hope to fix things, I arrived there unannounced and my father opened the door to me as though I had just popped out to the shops to grab some bread and milk after a day out. As though the thousands of terrible phone calls, the torrents of abuse, the death threats against Tin, had never occurred. But my father doesn't like to discuss things. He never has. As far as he was concerned, I was here, he welcomed me into the house. He did not hug me.

While my mum was relieved I was back – and I felt so much joy from seeing Savo again – my father was just the same. When I got there, I immediately knew nothing was going to be resolved. No pain was healed. There were no apologies from him. I walked around the big rambling mansion with feelings of both dread and numbness. And sure enough, within twenty-four hours he showed his true colours. He wanted control over me. He would not let me stay with my mother in her Belgrade apartment – I had to stay at his house instead. He didn't even allow me to go to the movies or to go for a walk in the city. I was twenty-two.

I was soon caught up again in his relentless search for public attention. He called a press conference with the Serbian media, and there the Dokic family was presented to the world as a happy unit, entirely defying the truth that we were emotionally fractured, bearing the scars and gaping wounds of decades of abuse.

It felt terribly wrong but I smiled awkwardly for the camera, told the press there were no hard feelings between my father and me. His big arm was draped over my shoulder – not as protection but as ownership. He had me back. It was fake, all for the press.

In the days afterwards, he continued to refuse to talk about any of the major issues between us. He framed the reason for my return as me having made a 'major mistake'.

A week later I left because I was emotionally breaking from being in his world again. It was way too hard and dangerous to tell him the truth – that I had to get away from him again – so I just told him I must go to Monaco and do some business but I'd be back in a couple of days. He was uncomfortable with me leaving but he didn't try to stop me. He did say, 'Make sure you send me $200,000 tomorrow.'

I agreed to.

He didn't say goodbye but I got hugs from my mum and Savo. On the journey to the airport I was in floods of tears as the emotional pain hit me in waves and I could feel the darkness creeping up again. I still couldn't understand why we couldn't work it out as a family, as a father and daughter.

I blamed myself.

The cycle

In the many years since then, I have tried one more time to mend things with my father and that also left me heartbroken and feeling like our failure to make any headway was my fault.

So what does that burden look like?

It means that for too long I've lived in a cycle of despair, numbness and self-loathing. I am the daughter of an abuser. And for long periods of my life I've felt unworthy of love. That I couldn't do enough, wasn't good enough to make my father love me properly; that is, as a parent should. That's how my father made me feel – worthless. I have never experienced the unconditional love that many parents give their kids.

I look at the last ten years of me trying to reinvent myself after being a tennis player. I have no idea how I did it, considering how badly I have habitually thought of myself. My self-loathing overpowered my thoughts nearly every day. A voice inside me said over and over, your own parents deserted you, and if they think so very little of you, then why would anyone else love you?

So I can do a great interview on court, do a keynote presentation, be applauded wildly, say thank you to those who have bought my book, listen to their stories, and have people appreciate me for things I've said and shown them about their own situations, but inside often I am feeling completely untethered. I have no confidence. And now I realise it's because actually I've never felt like I am good enough to be in these places, talking with apparent assurance to people who I am positive are much more comfortable and confident in themselves.

Though I have a great ability to compartmentalise, push through the fear and my insecurities to perform at a high level, in 2022 I realised it was time to seek professional help to start to fully heal and understand my past, and what that means for my future. And it was not until I started regular sessions with a psychiatrist around this time that I really began to dig deep, to begin to process the trauma of my childhood, youth and adulthood. As I've said, writing *Unbreakable* in 2016 was immensely helpful in that way and the start of healing, but it was only the beginning.

In the aftermath of my split with Tin, I sensed that I was spiralling and I needed to see a professional immediately.

My amazing friend Todd Woodbridge was the first I called after the split with Tin – at ten that same night. He picked up immediately, he listened to me – I was extremely upset, in tears, distraught. He managed to calm me down a little bit. He asked immediately if I would like to come and stay with him and his family. He suggested that I shouldn't be alone. I told him I would be fine to spend that night at my apartment, but I agreed I needed help – first thing in the morning. He contacted Tennis Australia straight away and between them they organised professional support the following morning.

So straight after that I began to talk to a psychiatrist, and he and I formed a good, solid bond from the start. I was in an emotional freefall, I was all over the place. But talking to this professional put me into a slightly better mindset, to the point that I felt capable of taking on the summer of tennis, which was beginning only three days later. Also, having Todd and the few people from Tennis Australia who knew what I was going through, and their support, really helped me in this tough time around Christmas, and enabled me to get on the plane and take up my commentary work that January.

Just as I embarked on the summer of tennis, and only a few days after Christmas and my break-up, I had put out a statement on Instagram announcing my separation from Tin. This was really forced on me because my management had found out that the media had got hold of the story and were going to run it in twenty-four hours. I thought it was better if I explained in my own words what had happened, so I put out the post. So as the summer rolled on, everybody knew.

As I headed into the busiest time of my year, doing commentary and TV work for five weeks, culminating in the Australian Open of 2022, privately I was shattered, but I managed to separate that from my work, and I turned up every day and gave 150 per cent. From a work perspective the five weeks were amazing, and I got the opportunity to finish off the summer by commentating the women's final, which saw Ash Barty win and lift the Australian Open trophy. It was a massive moment and a huge achievement; one that was a great honour for me to be able to witness, and call from the commentary box.

Todd and a few people from Tennis Australia had helped me immensely, as did the whole team at Channel 9. They were incredibly supportive: messages and phone calls came my way, offering me so much in the way of care. The director of Nine Sport, Brent Williams, and the head of Nine Tennis, Ben Clark, were instrumental in me feeling taken care of and supported.

But in the weeks after the Open ended, I could barely function. I was in my apartment building exhausted from the month – and without the distraction of the work my mind began to spiral.

This is how I found myself on a balcony again, in February 2022. And when this happened, it felt as though I was carrying the sum of all the pain and suffering I had been living with. It was my father beating me. It was my mum, I felt, not protecting me enough from him. It was Tin leaving on the eve of another Melbourne lockdown in mid-2021 and promising to return, but never coming back.

Yes, seventeen years on from me considering taking my own life in Monaco, I put myself in terrible danger again, first this time in February, then in March, and finally, the incident that most scared me, on 28 April 2022.

I was twenty-six floors up, in the apartment I'd shared until recently with Tin in inner-city Melbourne. On that day I remember looking down, and I could see myself jumping and landing on the ground. I was not scared. I thought to myself, if I am to do this, well, this would actually feel good because it's all done. I wouldn't have to deal with anything anymore. I felt this freeing feeling for five to ten seconds. It seemed like it would be a huge sense of relief. And that scared the shit out of me. Why? It felt way too good. It felt like I was on the cusp of freedom from all this pain. As I stood on the balcony, I was crying, because I could sense I was close to the end. There was nothing to live for.

Then I thought to text my psychiatrist. I told him that I needed to talk to him urgently.

He wrote back, 'I will call in ten seconds' and when he did I told him, 'I'm on the balcony and I want to jump.'

He was able to get me back inside, where I sat myself on the couch in floods of tears.

I was a mess. But he calmed me down.

Help

I soon found myself at Epworth Clinic, Melbourne, in a small room where I really started to unfurl some more of the most hellish times of my life. It was here, on a couch, that my focused journey to healing began.

While some may hold tight, keep quiet about what they find out about themselves in therapy, or perhaps even that they are getting counselling at all, I am going to share with you some of my learnings.

The reason why?

_____

I am sharing this in the belief that it may help you
if you or someone you know has suffered trauma.
I think it's really important to get professional help.
I thought for a long time that I could run away from
my problems and trauma but I know now that is
not possible.

_____

The professional I see is a calm man, and he always welcomes me into his office warmly. When we first sat down, I knew I was depressed, I explained that this black cloud had followed me around basically all my life since I'd made the decision to escape my family unit in the dead of night in Moscow all those years ago. While I was so much better after *Unbreakable* came out, and I had revealed the truth of my past, it was only the very start of healing. Healing can take a long time.

After my break-up with Tin, two days before Christmas 2021, it was clear I needed help. And through the sessions – particularly after my third incident on the balcony – my psychiatrist started to really dig into how my consciousness had been working. It was mind-blowing for me. He observed that I had PTSD. It was just as bad as my depression. He observed that I am always thinking the worst is going to happen and I live with a deep fear. I am constantly in a state of heightened anxiety.

I have been diagnosed with anticipatory anxiety, which means I am always expecting the worst. Say I have a flight tomorrow to Sydney, I think so darkly that I anticipate the plane crashing. Say I must travel to the coast, so I have to get into a car, I imagine we will be in an accident. I visualise these things happening to me. I don't even have to have a headache to worry that I might have a brain tumour. Or if there's a speaking engagement I really want to do, I anticipate the worst-case scenario: 'I'm not going to get it, or if I get it I'm going to screw it up. They'll fire me.'

I am always thinking something will go wrong. I live in a constant state of anticipating that the worst is going to happen.

In January 2022, I started an antidepressant. It is mild. I am talking about it here because I don't want people to feel shame about taking medication to treat mental health. Sometimes it is vital for your road to recovery. Everyone's recovery is unique, but for me it has really helped.

One of my psychiatrist's observations, at a session in June 2022, was a total revelation. He told me my self-worth was shot. It hit me like a thunderbolt. I knew my self-esteem wasn't great, but how bad it was became clear as he started to connect the trauma dots in my life.

He observed that I get a lot of my happiness from my work. That is, I feel good when I'm giving talks, addressing groups of people who may have suffered too. And then there is commentating – TV, I enjoy it, find it rewarding. Writing my books has been really important as well.

He also noticed that work is where I get my validation from, my confidence. That's right – he meant *all* of my self-validation and confidence come from my work, which, he told me, is a really emotionally fraught place to be.

Why am I like this? He explained that just as the tennis court used to be a place where, as a kid, I found some joy in my life, my work is doing the same thing for me these days. My talks, my book, they make me feel good and like I'm doing something valuable, helping people. They make me feel useful, as does my commentating.

So he enabled me to see that I was getting all my validation from outside of myself. It was all external. He explained that my work is so important for me because it's the only place where I feel I can really do some good or succeed. And, certainly in June 2022, and from way before then and to this present day, within my actual self I don't think I am good enough. In fact, at my worst I feel worthless.

The clincher for me was this: he told me that I was not taking any care of myself. He also told me in strong terms that I needed to *start* taking care of myself – that it should be my number one priority.

He laid it out: for a huge chunk of my life I was pre-occupied with making my father happy, be it by beating every local kid on the tennis court, climbing the rankings, beating a world No. 1, winning a WTA title, winning prize money, or handing over all the money I made in my career to my father. I just wanted to make him happy – so he would love me.

My psychiatrist said I needed to learn to find validation from within; that is, to be happy within myself. I had spent too long trying to make everyone else happy, but never myself.

How do I do that? I thought to myself. This was so foreign to me.

He said that I needed to start doing things where the priorities were me. He noted that people who have low self-esteem very often are those who don't look after themselves. And it all felt so true because I knew I'd been neglecting myself. I'm very good at taking care of others, but not myself.

He told me I'm quite traumatised from the past. It might shock you to hear this, but that was another revelation for me – that my past is why I've got so much fear around abandonment; why my self-worth is in pieces.

There was an awful night at Wimbledon in 2000, when something terrible happened after I had made the semi-finals of the grand slam. It has left a big scar of abandonment among other smaller ones. I had just played Lindsay Davenport. She was a great player, world No. 1 and a grand slam champion, and she was just too good in this match for me to beat her. I'd had an amazing run, I was only seventeen, it was a great result in such a celebrated tournament – a Wimbledon semi-final. But not in my father's eyes. After the loss, I couldn't find him. I called him. He wouldn't pick up for ages but I finally got through to him.

He was furious I'd lost. His voice boomed down the phone: 'You are pathetic, you are a hopeless cow, you are not to come home. You are a loser. Do not come back to the hotel.' Then he hung up. I slept in the grounds of Wimbledon.

Incidents like these fuelled my sense of unworthiness, and my anxiety – which by 2022 was at an all-time high. In the years since leaving my family unit, I'd lived with an incredible level of anxiety, all the time anticipating that something bad was about to happen, endless catastrophic ideas in my head. It was, and still can be, hard for me to see that good things will also come to me, even though I try really hard to believe they will. As my psychiatrist explained to me, that's all connected to anxiety, depression, trauma.

Learning to find hope

My psychiatrist said we have scars and they are always there. But in the same breath, he pointed out that when you are emotionally vulnerable, but open to learning, you can definitely absorb the tools, the methods, to cope with your trauma and start recovering.

He described life to me as a number of traumatic events from birth to death. Right? We're all going to experience them, whether it's a break-up, the death of a parent, losing a loved one. He says that it's important to accept this is a fact of living that we can't do much about. What we can control is how we deal with these difficult events in our lives when they occur. Brené Brown writes, 'You may not control all the events that happen to you, but you can decide not to be reduced by them.'

And so this is what I am trying to do now.

I'm trying not to run away from my trauma like I did before.

I'm not running away from it anymore because talking about it helps to get rid of some of those feelings. That's how you start to heal.

I have learnt I have a lot of fear about the future, but my psychiatrist pulls me up on my tendency to catastrophise, saying,

'There are options for you. Absolutely it's normal how you feel, but you are not thinking about all the options available to you, all the paths your life could take, which will likely be much more positive than the ones you are terrified of.'

He doesn't shame me about my negative thoughts; he reminds me that low self-esteem means we always think of bad outcomes. But these thoughts about bad outcomes are not reality. They are just thoughts. Which can, with effort, be controlled. So I'm trying to change some of my thinking, retrain my brain away from thinking so emotionally and towards thinking rationally.

Sometimes, when I walk into my therapist's office at the start of a session, I feel really depleted, but I always leave feeling stronger. One day a friend asked me how my psychiatrist makes me feel and I told her he makes me feel very, very calm. 'He has a calming voice, a reassuring tone,' I said. 'He makes me feel things are going to be all right. I feel like he has this ability to look at you and then show you what's going on.'

When I explained this to her, she said, 'He sounds like a caring parent.'

It was a total surprise to me, that observation.

'Yes, that's what a caring mum or dad does,' she said when I questioned this. 'The amount of times my parents as a kid or teen assured me, you've got this, it's going to be okay, things will get better, if I was having a hard time. And it's so obvious to me that you didn't have that.' And that really hit me. No, I never had that, but in a way, I do now.

I told my friend, 'If I didn't have my therapist in my life now, I am genuinely not sure I'd be talking to you.'

It's a devastating thought. But it is true. Therapy has saved my life.

Finally, there seems to be a way I am making sense of it all.

Our sessions fill me up with hope. I feel that things may get better even if it will take work and energy.

I will not be reduced by my past. I am here to heal, and opening up and talking about it all started it. Writing *Unbreakable* was the beginning; getting help has made me stronger, and is helping me thrive. Both are about releasing the pain. If it wasn't for both I wouldn't be here. You don't have to struggle in silence. You can live a great life with a mental health condition, but it's so important to open up to people so that you can get the help needed.

What I have learnt about mental health

- Don't be scared to get help from professionals. And it's never too late to do so.
- Some of the strongest people have battled mental health conditions.
- There is so much strength in being vulnerable.
- Being on medication is completely okay – there is no shame in it. Sometimes it can save you.
- Nine Australians suicide every single day. Almost a million people around the world suicide every year. These statistics show we need to have more open conversations about mental health. People are suffering in silence.

- People have gone from the darkest moments in their lives, to living their best life – it can be done and you can do it as well.
- You are so much more than a mental illness.

Mantra: Mental health illnesses don't define who you are. They are something you experience.

4.

DIAGNOSIS

*I think the biggest and the most important way
I have made a difference in my day-to-day
life has been finding help in the form of a
therapist. It unlocked so much
for me.*

I have thought long and hard about revealing what I am about to share with you. It's taken a lot of courage to get to this point, but with the way I'm living my life now, I feel compelled to do this. I want to share my life openly now.

In December 2022 I was diagnosed by my psychiatrist with traits of borderline personality disorder (BPD). I would like to help inform people about, and to also break the stigma around, this condition because it's not one that is spoken about often. Certainly not by people with a profile. So with that reason in my heart, I have decided to make public this difficult information I learnt from my psychiatrist at the end of a hard year.

I was left shocked when I was told. The diagnosis comes alongside ones of depression, anxiety and PTSD, which I also suffer as a result of my past.

When I was first informed I had some characteristics of BPD, I knew extremely little about the condition. In fact, when my psychiatrist first referenced the disorder, I immediately jumped to the conclusion that it centred around narcissism, a lack of emotion, not having any empathy for others. I was alarmed! But I also knew that wasn't me, so I was confused because I am the opposite – I have a lot of feelings and empathy that actually affect me emotionally. And I definitely know that I'm selfless.

It turns out my initial conclusions were very wrong. So, for those who don't know much about BPD, what is it and how does it manifest? The Australian government website Health-direct describes borderline personality disorder as affecting 'people's thoughts, emotions and behaviours, making it difficult for them to cope in all areas of life'.

'We all see the world through different eyes, but a person with borderline personality disorder has an abnormally distorted view of themselves and the environment around them,' it continues.

'People with borderline personality disorder feel intense, uncontrollable emotions, which can make them very distressed and angry. They have trouble with their relationships and find it hard to feel comfortable in themselves. They may be very impulsive and appear to lead chaotic lives, act impulsively or intentionally harm themselves as a way of coping.'

I was really surprised to learn that BPD is the most common personality disorder suffered in Australia – it affects 1 to 4 in every 100 people at some time in their lives; it's diagnosed more often in women, and usually the symptoms appear in the teenage years or early twenties.

Symptoms and behaviours of borderline personality disorder

- Feeling empty inside
- Low self-esteem
- Strong, overwhelming emotions and feelings
- Intense mood swings, including outbursts of anxiety, anger and depression
- A pattern of tumultuous relationships with friends, family and loved ones
- Alternating between idealising and devaluing other people
- Fear of being alone and frantic attempts to avoid abandonment
- Unstable and distorted self-image or sense of self
- Feeling neglected, alone, misunderstood, chronically empty or bored
- Feelings of self-loathing and self-hate
- Self-harm, such as cutting as a coping mechanism

- Suicidal thoughts or suicide attempts
- Impulsive and risk-taking behaviour, such as unsafe sex, illegal drug use, gambling, over-eating, reckless driving or over-spending
- Black and white thinking, or difficulty compromising
- Paranoid thoughts in response to stress
- Feeling cut off and out of touch with reality*

* healthdirect.gov.au/borderline-personality-disorder-bpd

My doctor has determined the way the BPD traits I have primarily manifest in my life is through shame, guilt, self-hate and self-sabotage. Also, fear of abandonment, low self-esteem, suicide attempts, feeling neglected. He has told me that this is the reason I have found myself mentally battling day to day for so long, and he's explained that I am suffering BPD because of my traumatic childhood, youth and adulthood.

Borderline personality disorder causes

There are lots of potential causes of borderline personality disorder. Under 'environmental factor', there are:

- Being a victim of emotional, physical or sexual abuse
- Being exposed to long-term fear or distress as a child
- Being neglected by one or both parents
- Growing up with another family member who had a serious mental health condition, such as bipolar disorder or a drink or drug misuse problem.

It will not surprise you to hear that these causes resonated with me, as they did with my psychiatrist. I'm told that 95 per cent of BPD sufferers can experience suicidal thoughts and addiction issues. For some the addiction might be alcohol, for others drugs, and some people can have issues with food, whether through binge eating or purging.

Of course, in my case it's my bingeing. It highlights my ability to self-sabotage. I have in the past shown remarkable discipline around what I put into my body, both during my career and after I retired, when I was determined to regain my physical fitness. I can stick to a plan and goal when I choose to. My comeback at the 2009 Australian Open is a case in point: I built myself back up from a bad place, fought my way into the main draw and emerged from tennis oblivion to take down some of the best players in the world and make the quarter-finals.

But just as I can create a constructive, ordered life, I can also tear it apart and quickly destroy any good work I have done or healthy systems I have put in place. This is all caused by self-hatred – very low self-esteem means that I do not feel I'm worthy of good things, which means I don't take care of myself.

It feels horribly painful to live like this.

Acceptance

When I was told of my traits of BPD, the diagnosis hit me hard. I knew I had depression, anxiety and PTSD, but this new, unfamiliar information made me reflect further on my often shame-filled existence up to this point. I would be lying if I said that the day I was told, I was not ashamed of the diagnosis.

I have become over the years a public figure who is proud to talk about mental health, who is constantly speaking about the value of opening up. I have shown my vulnerability through my first book, in interviews, on social media. And yet as I sat in that doctor's office in Melbourne in December 2022, the shame I felt meant my first instinct was to tell no one, not ever.

I was confused as to why I felt like that. But I can be very efficient at times when it comes to processing emotions and coming up with a plan. That feeling of deep shame lasted for about half a day. When I woke up the next morning, I felt an incredible amount of freedom. It surprised me! Something had lifted. The weight was off my shoulders. I felt liberation. I felt like, well, now I can actually work on this and get through it. Just as I was doing with decades of trauma.

I realised then that there's something empowering about being informed of what you have, what you're going through – because then you are able to work on it. To try to ease its effects. And I knew the diagnosis was going to help me understand more clearly my thought patterns and reactions to daily and life events.

The diagnosis has helped me so much already, because I'm doing a lot of work with my psychiatrist to understand the condition. And doing that enables me to be better at taking care of myself and going, okay, well, you know, this is where I get negative, this is why I panic. Now I can learn and recognise when and why these things are happening, and how to control them, and try to turn around and not let them control me. I understand it's going to take a lot of hard work but one thing is for sure, I am not afraid of that.

The day after my diagnosis, I thought to myself, I don't care what others think. I will talk about this openly. I will show my struggles and my scars, so it can help other people's healing. Maybe knowing what I'm going through will resonate with someone, so they don't feel like they're alone.

I know people may judge me for revealing so much about myself, but ultimately that says everything about them. If we all paid too much attention to people who didn't agree with how we live our life, it would be very paralysing.

Reflecting on the past

There's no doubt that as far back as my playing days, around my late teens, I felt something was not right in how I saw the world. I wonder now whether it was in those years, when I started to battle depression and anxiety, that my BPD traits were starting to manifest.

The stresses of my childhood weren't just because of the physical and emotional abuse I was surviving. It was also the fact that my early years were filled with escaping war and living in poverty and being bullied. And you know of how many times I was told or shown I was not good enough in my father's eyes. Let alone the violence. So while on the surface I loved every win, ticked every box as a competitor, turned up on time, played as hard as I possibly could, also I was broken.

I kept it together, remained stoic, not dealing with my feelings and thoughts with a professional or really anyone else close to me back then. Of course, that was detrimental to my mental health. However, I didn't realise the extent to which it was really falling apart. It's not like one day you just wake up and go, oh yeah, I have depression or anxiety. It was a slow awakening that something was wrong.

I knew this when, a year and a half after escaping home, I couldn't get out of bed to train. That had never happened before. I always liked to train and to play. Until I didn't want to do any of it. I didn't want to travel. As hard and as brutal as the tour is, and the relentless training, travel and competing it requires – most professional tennis players travel ten months of the year – until around that time travel had been something that I loved to do. But then everything came crashing down. I was exhausted. I was crying all the time. I couldn't keep everything inside anymore, suppress my distress.

These were my symptoms:

- Feelings and self-loathing and hate
- Shattered self-worth. I couldn't look at myself in the mirror
- Suicidal thoughts
- Fear of being alone and abandoned
- Heightened feelings of empathy for others

Privately, I have always been a highly sensitive person and for most of my life have felt that 'being sensitive' was a weakness. But what therapy has taught me is that being vulnerable and sensitive is a strength.

*Opening up the past and dealing with it to
move forward is one of the most powerful
moves you can make.*

Treatment

Borderline personality disorder is a condition that can be difficult for other people to understand. I know this first-hand because when my psychiatrist first uttered the words, as I've said, I was both scared and confused.

To help my symptoms, I was advised to start cognitive behaviour therapy (CBT). I had no idea what CBT was. In clinical speak, it's a type of therapy or talking therapy designed to enable you to develop healthy ways to cope with unhelpful thoughts. It teaches you skills to manage thinking that affects your moods, and using its methods you find new ways of reacting and behaving to replace harmful ones, and to think less negatively about yourself and your life. It helps you understand why you struggle with the things you do. Its main focus is to combat thoughts, feelings and behaviours that are affecting your quality of life.

My psychiatrist told me that after engaging with sessions of CBT I'd learn more fully how to accept who I am, how to regulate strong, unhealthy emotions and how to improve relationships, which is very important for me. He told me that the success of the CBT would rely on a strong relationship between me and him, that together we will try to take me to more of an understanding of myself and get rid of all that shame and guilt I collected in my childhood.

One thing I know to be true, and that I would say to others going through something similar, is that you must not give up on yourself. Also, and I've said it before but I want to empha- sise it: I think the biggest and the most important way I have made a difference in my day-to-day life has been finding help in the form of a psychiatrist. It unlocked so much for me.

Sure, I understand that you can feel shame around even going to see a therapist, let alone them giving you a mental health diagnosis. Initially, that can be shattering. But rather than being ashamed or embarrassed, for anyone who has endured this, we should be proud of trying to get through, survive and then ultimately overcome, so we can live happily, cherish our values, try to build up some self-worth, and under- stand how we function best (and worst).

I also understand how hard it is to find a therapist who is right for you, and that it can be an expensive process. A good thing can be to talk to your GP about referrals and what Medicare can cover for mental health sessions with a psychiatrist, a psycholo- gist or another kind of counsellor. As I found, sometimes it takes a while to find a mental health professional who is the right fit but it is really worth persisting until you do.

I think one big thing also is that a mental health diagnosis doesn't have to define who you are, but it can augment who you are. Fronting up to your mental health can make you stronger. It can make you more resilient. Some of the strongest people I know have gone through so much in the context of their mental health. It's important to understand why you're afraid, or why you're ashamed, or why you hate yourself. I am very confident that CBT will help me to unpack all these questions.

I know deep down that I'm a strong person and I am ready for this challenge – and that you are too.

A last word: listening to victim/survivors

I would like to say to those who want to help a friend or family member who is suffering: listen to their story. I appreciate it so much when people give me a safe space to talk about how I feel – they don't judge me or shame me, they simply listen. There is nothing more comforting as a survivor to have someone acknowledging your pain.

Perhaps the hardest aspect of being a survivor is the disbelief people will sometimes show for your story. It's hard to describe. I know that most of the time it's not that the people listening to you don't truly believe you. But still they say things like, 'How did that happen for so long?' For victim–survivors, phrases like that are upsetting. They are impossible for us to answer easily and they instil a note of doubt – are we believed? Did we do something wrong?

So if you're listening to a survivor entrusting you with their story, know we are doing it because we are crying out in pain. It's not to turn the spotlight on ourselves.

For many of us, sharing what happened to us is part of the process of healing from our pain. It's very important to know that it's *not* attention-seeking. People die because of this judgement every single day.

We are a society that judges, shames and stigmatises people for speaking up, but mourns and is shocked by deaths. This must stop – we must educate our communities to recognise and empathise with people who are struggling with their mental health, and to empower them by listening to them and encouraging them to seek help.

How to be a good friend to someone who has a mental illness

- Check in on them regularly
- Listen to what they have to say without judgement
- Create a positive and supportive environment
- Be patient
- Educate yourself if you don't understand
- Show them and tell them how much they mean to you and how much you love them
- Encourage them positively

Mantra: Being vulnerable is powerful – confronting your past can lead to healing.

5.

THE MEDIA

*'It is so important for our nation – the whole world,
in fact – to listen to survivors' stories. Whilst
they're disturbing to hear, the reality of what goes
on behind closed doors is more so. And the more
details we omit for fear of disturbance, the more we
soften these crimes, the more we shield perpetrators
from the shame that is resultantly misdirected to
their targets.'*
Grace Tame, National Press Club address,
March 2021

I wasn't fearful of the media, or nervous with them, as a young person. I can't recall my first-ever interview but I do remember I was comfortable being quizzed by journalists during my rise through the junior tennis ranks.

One of my first big newspaper interviews was in 1998 with *The Age* and I spoke about my career and what I hoped

I could be. I also made appearances on the *Today* show and, while I spoke shyly, I didn't show a hint of nerves.

But as my tennis career took off, my relationship with the media changed. I was perceived as cold by some and a bit of a 'brat' by others. While some journalists noticed my sad eyes, as a result of my father's behaviour my relationship with the media was unquestionably impacted.

In *Unbreakable*, I wrote about the pain of being trapped in an awful cycle where I did not have a voice and my father's views were perceived to be mine. Around the time of my rise, through 1999, 2000 and 2001, it was impossible to miss the way journalists tended to relish his crazy performances. Damir Dokic, the 'tennis dad from hell', was a headline writer's dream back then. My father became a walking punchline and a joke to others. Though it was obvious he was an angry and volatile character, no one stopped to reflect on this too much. But he was aggressive and drunk and publicly a mess, so I always struggled to understand why there wasn't more commentary of 'Well, you know, there's something clearly wrong with this guy – we should be concerned that this man's a father in charge of his daughter. There are two young children living with this person.'

You can't forget that my father did a lot of interviews with the media when he was drunk. The US Open, in 2000, is a case in point. Over the course of half an hour he made a big drama about the price of fish at a tournament café. He called WTA chief executive Bart McGuire 'a gangster', and kept yelling, 'Fucking US Open' and 'Fucking WTA'.

'The USA country doesn't have a heart, they have cold concrete,' he screamed outside Flushing Meadows, the US Open grounds. 'I'm never coming back to this place – it's too dirty and too communist.'

There's footage of us after this debacle. His big arm over my shoulder. Me distraught, as a US Open courtesy van drives us back to the hotel. I am silent through it all, trying not to trigger him any more and just get him out of public view. In old photographs and video you can see the trauma etched on my face. I have tears streaming down my face. I look frightened.

In hindsight I find it bizarre that nobody wrote a blazing article questioning, should we be concerned here? Is that girl okay? What about her welfare? She has a little brother – how is he? What is actually going on? Instead, his drunken and aggressive behaviour was glorified.

If you go through the clippings around this time, the articles focus on my father over and over again. They talk about his abuse of tournament officials, security guards, hotel staff, police, journalists themselves, but it doesn't seem to occur to anyone to ask if I, or Savo, who was eight years younger, were traumatised or embarrassed by whatever our father was doing now to attract the wrong kind of attention. Or what might be happening away from the spotlight of the press's attention. After the US Open incident, there was a *New York Post* article that described all the trouble he'd caused, at the US Open and other tournaments, and then its last two lines stated: 'Jelena has always defended her dad. "I like having him around," she said earlier this summer.'

Reading coverage like this, it's hard not to feel angry. No wonder back then I saw the media as a tool for my father – who

used newspaper and TV reporters to amp up his own noto-
riety. And they seemed all too happy to comply. When I was
playing at Wimbledon in 2001, going into my fourth-round
match against Austrian player Barbara Schett, the *Daily
Mirror* ran the headline 'BABSI v. THE BEAST'. It referred to
my opponent and my father. It was incredibly hard to focus
knowing these toxic articles were being written: 'It is billed as
the battle between Beauty and the Beast. *Mirror* girl Barbara
Schett, 25, faces Jelena Dokic on one of Wimbledon's show
courts today. But the "beast" she will be facing comes in the
shape of Jelena's overbearing dad Damir.'

My invisibility in these articles was, and remains, distress-
ing. Another hurtful headline – remember, I was eighteen at
the time and my brother was ten – referenced the hotel I was
staying at as a brothel. What kind of an editor puts out a newspaper story like that – about two young kids?

After the release of *Unbreakable* in November 2017, journalist Claire Harvey, then at the *Sunday Telegraph*, reflected on
the role of the media in calling out abuse:

> If you have an uncomfortable feeling while you're reading
> Jelena Dokic's harrowing accusations of abuse against her
> father today, stop and ask yourself what that feeling might
> be. Revulsion? Sure. Me too. Guilt? I hope so. Because Aus-
> tralians, collectively, failed this little girl . . . For most of us,
> Damir Dokic was a clown; a bad joke. For his daughter, he
> was a monster; a violent abuser who once beat her uncon-
> scious – and the most frightening thing of all was that
> Jelena Dokic knew nobody was coming to save her.

Some journalists have apologised to me privately, some publicly, about using my father as the means to get a story, and about not questioning the effects his behaviour was having on our family. I appreciate that. I understand that reporting and investigating abuse can be complex. But still, it's impossible not to look back and wish more had been done to support me during that time. And even more so after I separated from my father.

I believe that all the major media companies should run modules for their journalists on educating them on abuse culture. I think the hard stories must be told – they are so important to changing the culture and journalists need to be trained on how to talk to survivors and tell these stories. If they don't understand it, they need to be educated on it. They should never be thinking of abuse as a means to get a headline, especially where young people are concerned.

I hope that nowadays, after so many reckonings and bad stories have come out, reporters would cover an abuse story with much more care and consideration than they did mine. And I hope that they would more deeply question concerning behaviour in their articles. Certainly, after *Unbreakable* was published, there was some thoughtful, empathetic reporting about my book and what I'd been through. Richard Hinds, writing for what was then Fairfax Media, stated:

As a sports writer who regularly covered the grand slam tournaments throughout Dokic's career, we all knew something was wrong with the Dokic family. Even if our suspicions did not touch the surface of the horrendous abuse now revealed. The erratic, often drunken public outbursts of Damir Dokic created obvious concerns ...

I can remember three separate occasions when myself, or a colleague, raised this allegation with TA. The response was similar to that given by TA on Sunday after the release of Dokic's book. 'There were many in tennis at the time who were concerned for Jelena's welfare, and many who tried to assist with what was a difficult family situation,' the statement said. 'Some officials even went as far as lodging police complaints, which without cooperation from those directly involved, unfortunately could not be fully investigated.' The unofficial version of this statement was this: 'We've heard all the stories. But if Jelena doesn't speak up, we can't do anything.' In the light of Dokic's revelations this lightfooted approach seems unjustifiable, even unforgivable.

And since then, segments of the media, both TV and newspaper journalists and commentators, have really got behind me and supported me and my advocacy work. I appreciate that very much.

Ultimately, I feel strongly that there needs to be more kindness and empathy from all sides of the media.

On my publicity tour for *Unbreakable* in 2017, there was a group of journalists who were thoughtful and sensitive and not wanting to upset me. They were amazing. There was another group who even after reading the book didn't seem to quite understand what I was talking about. In fact, some appeared to struggle to even fathom I had been through this and survived.

I get this is a difficult subject for people to tackle. I understand that. Which is why I want to talk about it and keep talking about it. I hope the media can work more effectively to make survivors feel safe enough to tell their stories because it's incredibly important to destigmatise this issue in order to help people suffering.

Using my voice for change

In late October 2022, horrifying footage emerged of an attack by an adult on a teenager on the tennis court in Serbia. Anti-violence advocate Igor Juric – he fights hard for children's rights and safety – first posted the clip that showed a fourteen-year-old girl returning to the side of the court with her father during a training session in Belgrade, Serbia, where the man kicked and hit the girl, before he threw her to the ground and kicked her again.

The footage, his actions, were extraordinary and gut-wrenching. When I saw the clip, I threw up. It was triggering but it also moved me to ask some questions on social media.

Dokic_Jelena ✅

You think this is brutal?

It is but it's a normal day for a lot of us that have been or are abused especially as children.

Hitting, ear pulling, spitting in our faces, throwing us on the ground, punching and kicking us. Just another day for us and that includes this 14-year-old girl.

Imagine what happens behind closed doors. It's even worse.

This is exactly why I spoke up about this and wrote about it.

I always said I am not the first or the last to go through this but my question now is have things changed in the way our sport and society deals with this?

I am glad this monster was caught on video but people are watching this and not doing anything until he started kicking her on the floor.

Also, the media needs to do more.

Talk about this more. Our sport and players especially the ones that have a large platform need to raise awareness around this.

And clubs, federations, governing bodies need to do their part. This is where they now need to step up.

The question is whether enough is being done even just raising awareness about this.

All the journalists around the world and all of you on your Twitter profiles who love all the stories and gossip, how about this?

Are some players playing a grand slam or not or are they dating each other?

Who cares. How about this poor girl.

Who will talk about her and protect her?

I will tell you from personal experience. **Nobody.**

I just hope that this time around someone will
help because she is scared and broken and she
will be traumatised forever.

Come on everyone, media, social media, players,
ex players, journalists . . . please share this, talk
about this, post it, repost it.

It's tough to watch?

Yes but don't forget that the reality of what goes
on behind closed doors is even more brutal.

Because don't forget not everyone survives
this and lives are lost because of this type of
behaviour that we don't talk about enough.

Some don't survive, some are killed and some
take their own lives.

You just don't hear about it.

So it's time to make some noise.

As this crisis was unfolding I immediately thought, okay, we need to talk about this, we need to shed light on this issue, we need to give it the space and attention it actually needs.

A number of media outlets contacted me, including the *Today* show, whose host, Karl Stefanovic, wanted to speak with me. On the program I made a statement and asked what more could be done to protect children and young people in tennis. 'It was just sickening to watch, as someone who's been through it,' I said to Karl. I suggested we could have an anonymous platform to get help, and asked, 'Who is looking after these kids? Someone needs to be responsible for the wellbeing of these young kids.'

This man should never be allowed near a tennis court again, but unfortunately many before him who have acted this way have got away with it.

I was not alone in expressing my rage.

Some other members of the tennis community also reacted.

Pam Shriver wrote, 'OMG we all need to report and press charges against this kind of horrible abuse.'

In the days after the video was made public, the man behind the assault on the teen girl in Serbia was charged by local police. Serbia's Ministry of Internal Affairs announced a Chinese citizen had been arrested over the incident:

> 'After a video of him (allegedly) beating his 14-year-old daughter appeared in the media, the police immediately took all measures and actions within their jurisdiction and quickly identified the suspect,' the ministry said in a translated statement. '[The man] was ordered to be detained for up to 48 hours and he will be brought to the First Basic Public Prosecutor's Office in Belgrade with a criminal report.'

Investigative articles about abuse in sport are so important – they really can make a big difference. In this case, the media coverage around this disgusting assault finally led to the man's arrest, but it took some time for the coverage to start. As I wrote on Instagram, 'I am told that this footage has been circulating around for a few weeks in the tennis community and that many people, parents and coaches knew about this. I am also told that this is not the first time and that this girl has been abused like this in public for a few weeks now in front of people and nothing has been done. How many more assaults are happening that no one is covering or taking seriously?'

We still don't know if this man will be allowed back on a tennis court. But with the way tennis is loosely regulated in some countries, I would not be a bit surprised if he was. It's the 'win at all costs attitude' that still pervades sport that is the problem. The pursuit of success can make people blind to suffering. People don't call out shocking behaviour because of money and winning. It is as simple as that. And this is the culture of many sports, as has been proven repeatedly in recent years. Another example is British gymnastics. In July 2020 a group of British gymnasts wrote an open letter on Twitter, the main thrust of their words being that abuse in their sport is 'completely normalised'. Emotional and physical abuse were simply accepted.

Following their revelation on social media, an independent review found that British gymnastics enabled a culture where young competitors were starved, body-shamed and abused in a system that ruthlessly put the pursuit of medals over the protection of children.

A message to the media

I love being part of the media now, giving my opinions and thoughts. I have many friends in the media, including journalists, and I believe things have changed since I was in the eye of those storms twenty years ago. As I've said, I hope that today my story would not be covered the way it was back then. But I still come across some foolish and irresponsible journalists. A case in point: in 2021, while all the players taking part in the Australian Open were compulsorily isolating in their hotel rooms before the tournament, I was asked during an interview by a media personality whether I could relate to being confined to one room. I wasn't sure what this person was getting at, but was gobsmacked when in the next sentence they expanded on what they meant, saying surely I could relate to not having proper toilet facilities because I'd grown up during a war and become a refugee. They laughed about it. I was disgusted at this line of questioning. This is why still in the 2020s we can't trust the media all the time. They can always be more rigorous and kind, especially to young athletes, and they need to be ready and educated to communicate difficult, uncomfortable stories. In September 2022, French player Fiona Ferro spoke out against her former coach, leading to him being charged with raping and sexually assaulting her when she was a teenager. She also called on the media to do more to uncover incidences of abuse in tennis: 'I think it's your guys' job also . . . to do the research, to help people to open up more. Hopefully one by one try to eliminate that type of situation.'

And it's important to cover these stories properly – that is, sensitively, in a way that empowers survivors rather than bringing on shame for them. If journalists are not reporting the news responsibly, they are letting down the survivors and not changing the system. In January 2023 a headline about Pam Shriver's advocacy stated: 'Tennis players must stop having sex with their coaches'. Jane Gilmore, who runs a website called FixedIt, which examines the way abuse and sexual violence cases are handled in newspaper headlines, rewrote it as: 'Pam Shriver says tennis leaders should protect teenage players from sexually abusive coaches.' Gilmore said:

Words are amazing and powerful things. They're what we use to communicate how we feel and what we think. The people who wrote, edited, approved, and published this headline appear to be communicating that they think teenage girls are responsible for the choices made by men twice their age who abuse their position of power to damage girls and young women.

Japanese tennis great Naomi Osaka has called out the way the media treats players during press conferences. Sometimes these conferences can get aggressive, with reporters throwing out personal or provocative questions that players don't want to answer. But there is tons of pressure to respond to every single question at a press conference. Osaka made the point that sometimes she didn't want to attend press conferences for the sake of her mental health, but if she didn't the media would write unpleasant pieces about her absence. She said, 'I felt under a great amount of pressure to disclose my symptoms – frankly because the press and the tournament did not believe me. I do not wish that on anyone and hope that we can enact measures to protect athletes, especially the fragile ones . . . I ask the press for some level of privacy and empathy next time we meet.'

I've had all sorts of questions thrown at me at press conferences, especially about my father, even when it was clear I was really distraught, even in tears. What also hurt me was the fact that after I'd escaped home and distanced myself from my father and his views, the media continued to cover stories about me as though nothing had changed. No matter how far I had stepped away from him – had no outbursts, no incidents, was always open with reporters – they still didn't really give me a chance; it seemed as though nothing had changed in their eyes. It ruined my reputation for the rest of my playing career and for fifteen more years – it didn't shift until *Unbreakable* came out.

I would also strongly encourage the media to have empathy towards young athletes because in a lot of sports we are thrown in at the deep end with expectation and pressure when we are still, really, children. Girls, sometimes as young as fourteen, are dealing with this.

Media has a big reach and impact so it's important to try to use it for good. I would hate anyone to suffer like I did, to have their abuser's behaviour glorified and turned into what today is known as 'clickbait'. Personally, when I think of all the support I've had from various journalists and outlets in the past few years, I feel incredibly grateful that they have taken such positive steps to understand my story, to get behind me. But we all need to be vigilant and really careful, over and over again, with those who are suffering.

_____

Mantra: the media should not under any circumstance shame or stigmatise or victim-blame. When we see this happening we must call it out.

_____

6.

SOCIAL MEDIA AND COMMUNITY

I am grateful for my Instagram community; it has
supported me in many of my hard days and times.
I just hope I can do the same for all my supporters.
My Instagram community is my family and I want
them to think of me in the same way.

For decades I was stuck in my father's shadow because the
media was always talking about him, always looking for headlines, and even when I left home and had disengaged from
him, they kept talking about him. I was referred to in newspaper articles and feature pieces as 'Jelena Dokic, the daughter
of Damir Dokic'.

Decades ago, in press conferences I came across as a quiet,
sullen person. I was saying whatever my father pressured me
to say. But around the time *Unbreakable* was released in 2017

I was in the process of well and truly reclaiming my voice and this is when I discovered Instagram.

I was a little bit terrified at first of the social media app because I knew someone will always have an opinion. Of course people are allowed to have different views from mine, and that's fine, but I was afraid specifically of bullying because of my past. My feelings of being 'socially unacceptable' in part have been fuelled by the bullying I went through as a kid at primary school and high school in Fairfield. I was teased for my appearance, for a small mole I had on my face; my classmates called me 'mole face'. It was compounded by the experience I felt in my first years of junior tennis in Australia, where I had an overwhelming feeling of not belonging, of being left out. This happened not just with other junior players, but also their parents – I overheard one of the tennis mothers saying, 'I wish they would go back to where they came from.' On another occasion, on an overseas tour, when I made an attempt to take part in a card game with the rest of my tennis team in a team-mate's room, I was greeted with, 'Go back to where you came from' and had the door slammed in my face.

So with Instagram, I didn't really know what I was getting into, but I thought, I'll try it and if I don't like it or if it gets too much, then I'll pull the pin. I hoped it would be a space where I could be creative.

I've never regretted being on Instagram – I love my community.

I didn't expect it would become somewhere I could be so open and honest, and own my voice. Most of all, it is a community where I can gain strength when I am feeling down. And it's not just a community that is supportive of me – I can see it's a place where people are supporting each other, and hopefully where I can support them as well.

So I have found interacting with people on Instagram is really meaningful, and I've taken a lot of strength and comfort from those who message me, and are kind. My social media community has absolutely got me through some horrendous times in my life, especially as I struggled with my relationship breakdown with Tin, which I'll speak about later.

At the low point in April 2022 that I talked about earlier, when I was extremely fragile and struggling a lot with my mental health, I wrote:

Dokic_Jelena ✅

Everything is blurry. Everything is dark.

No tone, no picture, nothing makes sense . . .
just tears, sadness, depression, anxiety and pain.

The last six months have been tough.

It's been constant crying everywhere. From
hiding in the bathroom when at work to wipe
away my tears so that nobody sees it to the
unstoppable crying at home within my four walls
has been unbearable.

Constant feelings of sadness and pain are just not going away and my life has been shattered.

I blame myself, I don't think I am worthy of loving and I am scared.

I also know that I still have so many things to be grateful for and then I start to hate myself because by feeling this way I feel like I am not grateful because I mustn't be since I want to end it all.

Such a vicious cycle in my head.

The result: almost jumping off my 26th floor balcony on April 28th.

Will never forget the day, I just wanted the pain and the suffering to stop.

I pulled myself off the edge, don't even know how I managed to do it. Getting professional help saved my life.

This is not easy to write but I have always been open, honest and vulnerable with you all and I deeply believe in the power of sharing our stories to help us get through things and to help each other.

I am writing this because I know I am not the only one struggling.

Just know that you are not alone.

I am not going to say that I am doing great now but I am definitely on the road to recovery. Some days are better than others and sometimes I take a step forward and then a step back but I'm fighting and I believe I can get through this.

I believe in the following:

it's ok to feel what I am feeling.

It's ok to feel sad just keep fighting and come back.

That's what I am trying to do and that's what keeps me going.

Don't be ashamed of what you are feeling.

It's ok to feel this way and you can come back from it. It's possible, just keep believing.

Love you all and here is to fighting and surviving to live and see another day.

I will be back stronger than ever

Underneath my post people I knew, and many I didn't know, wrote imploring me not to give up, saying they were there for me. I was struck by the outpouring, from friends such as former tennis player Mark Philippoussis to the model Megan Gale to endurance athlete and motivational speaker Turia Pitt, a woman who has gone through so much and is an inspiration to me. They were all telling me they stood with me.

I was stunned by these outpourings of love. When you're enduring something so hard and you see so many amazing people reaching out to you, it's uplifting.

After I posted, I also had messages saying things like, 'Look, I don't know you personally, but, you know, I'm sending you a message saying I am a huge supporter of yours, please hold on, just call me now.' 'We'll go out for a walk along the Yarra.' 'I can meet you for coffee.'

Unquestionably, there are downsides to social media. I've talked about them, and we've all experienced them: the bullying, the abuse and the mean comments. But that day, and many others, there was nothing but love and generosity.

The most common private and public messages I receive from people are thank yous: 'Thank you for sharing your story and your hard days.' 'Thank you for sharing the hard things that you go through.' 'Thank you for sharing because I now know I'm not the only one going through hard things, you make me feel less alone.' 'You make me feel like I have a voice.' 'You make me feel heard.' 'You make me feel like there is hope.'

Social media has given me a voice and reinforced that there is power and strength in being vulnerable – and most importantly that my honesty about my battles can help others.

In a positive social media community . . .

- Alone we can change lives, together we can change the world.
- Community gives a sense of belonging and there is nothing more powerful than feeling like you belong somewhere.
- Community equals a safe environment, a safe space united together where we can be ourselves and not be shamed or embarrassed.
- With my Instagram family I want to build a supportive community, where people can find inspiration, help, hope and empowerment, especially in the tough moments; where you can be your most open self and vulnerable with no shame. That is what connection and support is, that's when change happens.

Below are some of the posts that have resonated and impacted a lot of people – and, I hope, given them inspiration and a conversation around difficult issues.

On 6 April 2023 I posted about domestic violence and speaking up:

Dokic_Jelena ✅

Swollen, bruised and bleeding shins from being beaten and kicked all night with sharp shoes right into my shins for losing a match.

These images were taken more than 2 weeks later and I was still heavily bruised.

I was 17 years old.

To this day I still have sensitive and bumpy shins from this beating.

From every wound there is a scar and these are mine. I have survived but not everyone, woman and girl, has or will.

And that's the sad reality.

Why this post?

I was speaking at a Domestic and Family Violence event today and I was sad.

Sad and angry for the tens of millions of women out there in the world who I know right in this moment are going through a lot worse than I ever did.

1 woman a week is killed from domestic violence in Australia alone.

1 in 4 women will experience domestic violence in their lifetime.

The figures are even worse around the world.

The more that we don't talk about it, the more we shy away from the issue, the more we are abandoning women and girls.

For those reading this that might be experiencing abuse or domestic violence just know I get you.

I know how scared and afraid you are.

Know that you have incredible strength and courage.

Nothing is your fault.

For those that can please be there for those that need help and support. Don't shy away from them and don't abandon them.

Coming from someone that has been there, abandoned and scared to death please don't turn your back. Women and girls need you and your help.

SPEAKING UP ABOUT DOMESTIC VIOLENCE IS NOT ATTENTION SEEKING.

WOMEN AND GIRLS DIE EVERY DAY BECAUSE OF THIS JUDGEMENT AND SHAME.

AND WHEN IT HAPPENS IT'S UNFORTUNATELY TOO LATE.

WE LIVE IN A SOCIETY THAT SHAMES AND STIGMATISES TALKING ABOUT ABUSE AND DOMESTIC VIOLENCE BUT THEN WE MOURN THE KILLINGS DUE TO VIOLENCE.

Let's do more for the future generations. For our daughters, sisters and all the girls and women around the world to make this a better and safer place for them to be happy, healthy and free of violence.

I will never stop fighting and speaking up about this issue especially for those that can't and don't have a voice.

On 4 April 2023 I posted a message framed as one to my younger self, to remind my community about our self-worth, about our strength:

Dokic_Jelena ✔

What would I say to my younger self?

To this young, already sad and scared girl,

Never let anyone put you down.

Never let anyone tell you that you can't do something.

Never let anyone disrespect you.

Never let anyone shatter your self worth.

Don't let anyone knock you down.

Keep your head up.

Believe in yourself.

Never give up.

Always continue fighting.

Never let anyone take away your voice.

Don't let anyone take away your light.

Be fearless.

You are stronger than you think.

You can do anything.

You can get through anything.

You have courage and bravery inside you that can get you through even when you are scared half to death.

Be kind to yourself.

Have love for yourself.

You deserve the world.

DON'T YOU EVER LET ANYONE TAKE AWAY YOUR HAPPINESS BECAUSE IT WAS NEVER THEIRS TO TAKE.

Now I am going to stick this on my fridge and my bathroom mirror so that I can remind myself every single day that I am worthy and those that tried to break me didn't succeed and they made me what I am today.

And that is unbreakable and fearless.

STRONGER THAN EVER.

And this goes to anyone out there that needs to hear this right now.

Just know, you deserve the world.

Believe it.

Love you all,

Jelena xoxo

On 29 March 2023, I wanted to talk again about body-shaming and self-image:

Dokic_Jelena ✅

Let's talk about body shaming!

Nobody should be body shaming and scrutinising anybody's body. PERIOD.

While I could talk about this subject all day, I will just make two points:

1. Just because someone else sees our bodies as nothing else but a size number or how we look in a bikini, it has nothing to do with our capabilities and our worth. If it did then that would mean that being a size 2 for example would be ok even if we were a bully or a mean person. It wouldn't matter as long as we are a size 2.

But if we were a size 18 but a good, kind, generous person who works hard, who has good morals and values and does good in the world, well that wouldn't matter because that person is a size 18 so they deserve to be judged and made fun of.

How bad is that?

2. And the second thing is, if we really are good and kind human beings and really concerned about other people then just stop commenting on their bodies, weight and appearance.

What message are we sending to the younger generation if this is ok and if we act this way.

Not a good one that's for sure.

So be kind.

Size doesn't matter. It doesn't define someone's worth.

And by the way, people can always lose a bit of weight and they can get a bit fitter but those that body shame, they will always be unkind people.

I am a size 16. Yes I am.

So does that mean I am a bad person?

Does that define my worth?

Do I deserve to be looked at differently compared to someone that is a size 2?

Definitely not.

All that matters is that I am a good, hard working, kind, empathetic and generous human being.

Please don't judge or mock others based on their weight. It's not nice.

Be kind everyone.

A few days before this, I wanted to highlight the importance of authenticity for me:

Dokic_Jelena ✔

Alright, keeping it real with this unflattering photo in the plane going back home after a massive few weeks and with my double chin and all.

I think it's important to be real, authentic and honest and to show the good and the sometimes not so good.

And that's what I want to do.

It's been a huge day as has this whole year already.

Woke up at 4 am, car to the airport, flight from Melbourne to Sydney, car to my event in Sydney, change from my travel clothes into my event outfit, do my hair and makeup, had my heels on for 4 hours, keynote presentation plus a Q&A for an hour, lunch with the guests, rush to get changed into my travel clothes, take my makeup off in the car back to Sydney airport, fly back to Melbourne, get in the car and get home asap because I have to be up at 7 am to go to another speaking conference tomorrow.

So it's been 16 hours, I am tired, hair is up in a bun, makeup off as I couldn't have it on my face any longer, my eyes are closing, all my brain is thinking about is a hot shower and bed.

Why this post?

Because for me it's important to show it all and life is not always sunshine and rainbows.

Even though I am very happy, satisfied and as I like to call it 'grateful tired' and I had an amazing day and an amazing event with wonderful people, I still had a hectic day and I am exhausted

And that's ok.

I can't wait for my pumpkin soup, hot shower and bed tonight. That is my recharge which is so important.

So while I do work hard and I have a crazy busy schedule most of the time, I do try and balance it the best that I can.

So after my big day tomorrow, I get two days off which I will spend with friends, get some sleep and binge watch some Netflix.

It's all a balance, life is balance.

I am not saying I have it all figured out but I try my best.

So the conclusion is:

– it's not easy and that's life and I want to be honest about the good and the bad so if anyone out there is struggling they can find some comfort knowing they are not alone, including looking like crap

– try to give yourself some time to rest and just know
    you are doing so well just by showing up every single
    day and some days will be tougher than others.

Love you all,

Jelena xoxo

I think it's important to commemorate certain days of the
year when I post. On this one from October 2021 I attached
a photo of me looking miserable and stressed at a press conference when I was seventeen. In the post I wanted to talk
about an important date for me:

Dokic_Jelena ✅

WORLD MENTAL HEALTH DAY!!

This photo brings up a lot of sadness and pain
and was taken during a period of my life where I
was experiencing depression, anxiety and PTSD.
Only a few years later I almost ended my life.

Today I am in such a different space.

Having gone through many personal challenges
and come out the other side, I know how
important it is to check in on people around you.

I know that not everyone is fortunate enough to
get through difficulties like I have.

That's why today is so important to raise awareness
globally of mental health issues and mental illness.

It might not seem like a big deal but for anyone facing mental health struggles, just knowing that someone cares for you really does make a world of difference.

I know how important it is to check in with family, friends or anyone struggling.

I struggled immensely and wish more people would have checked in on me.

So please show support and be kind because you never know what someone is going through and what battle they are fighting.

Sometimes people underestimate the power of sending a text or making a phone call. It doesn't take a lot of time and effort and it might not seem like a big deal but it really can and does have an enormous impact. I know it always has and does for me.

On every level, we need to have more open conversations about mental illness.

So take care of yourself and take care of others on this very important global day.

There is a lot we can do for ourselves as well as others:

— Call friends, family and those struggling and tell them you're thinking of them.

– Send a bunch of flowers to someone who
might be struggling.

– Write down what you're grateful for.

– Look after your body and try to be active.

– Reach out for professional help if you need it.

Sending you all so much love and especially to
those out there struggling. Just know that you
are not alone.

If you or anyone you know needs help, contact
Lifeline on 13 11 14.

A word on mental health and trolling

I've spoken about the darker side of social media. A part
of that which always shocks me is the hate members of the
sporting community, including some tennis players, receive
on their socials after matches. Madison Keys, who reached
the Australian Open semi-finals in 2022, told CNN a few
years before that, 'I don't think people realise, for all these
matches we get death threats.' Her experiences pushed her to
promote awareness of cyberbullying through a partnership
with FearlesslyGirl, an organisation that promotes leadership
for young women.

Todd Woodbridge was forced to call out a terrible, abusive
message he was sent during the 2023 Australian Open. After
he'd talked about a mild heart attack he'd suffered a few
months before, he found this on his socials: 'Just a old has been

trying to stay in the lime light! Shame they [*sic*] heart attack didn't end you.'

As I told Todd then, we're all behind him – we must call out these trolls and expose them. I was so angry to see that message, knowing how scared Todd had been after the heart attack. What kind of people get a kick from posting this hate?

Around the same time, I was being body-shamed on Instagram and other social media platforms, and then I received online abuse about my mental health. In among this I was asked if I was going to try to kill myself again – punctuated with a laughing emoji.

This kind of abuse is unspeakably vile. I wonder if these people just don't know how harmful such words can be, or perhaps they just don't care. I called out the post, writing,

> What kind of a person can write something like this and then even worse laugh about it? A bad person, that's who. And of course an ignorant one. I am thinking of all of those who have committed suicide, those who have wanted to, those who have lost friends and loved ones to suicide and all those struggling. I am fighting for all of those who feel like they don't have a voice . . . So many are at their absolute breaking point so please be kind, caring and understanding. Sending so much love to all the good people out there and especially to all those struggling.

Twenty-four hours later, a woman wrote to me thanking me for speaking up. Her brother had suicided only a couple of days earlier, and his family had had his funeral the night before she wrote to me. A family had been devastated because of losing one of their own to suicide. The most terrible loss, and yet people out there are actually joking about it. How can this happen? When someone tells you to kill yourself, you wonder how they can even *think* of saying that, let alone writing to someone to say it. And how can we have a platform that allows that?

Social media companies need to enforce a better, safer standard on these platforms. It's hard for me to emphasise enough how much I would like these companies to do better to make their spaces safer.

If I was playing on Rod Laver Arena and someone was abusing me and yelling the things they write to me on social media, that person would be arrested. This happens only so occasionally with social media abuse.

So, how do social media organisations make people accountable for this kind of behaviour? Should they ban anonymous accounts? Verify every new account by requiring, for example, users enter personal details from a driver's licence or another kind of ID, so there is no hidden trolling? I am not sure whether it would be successful but it's definitely something worth discussing. Nor do I think any one person should be able to open multiple accounts under different names, and maybe verifying accounts to an individual who's had to prove their identity would help to prevent that happening.

Calling it out

I'm pleased to see there is an e-safety commissioner in Australia whose purpose is to aim for positive experiences online. They have a lot of work to do in this space. Also, in July 2020 the government formed a national sports integrity commission, Sport Integrity Australia. It's designed to protect the sport we play in Australia and look after those who are involved in clubs at an amateur and professional level. At the end of 2022 the commission decided to do some research into cyberbullying. Its CEO said that the project is 'vital to help stem the scourge of online abuse directed at sportswomen'. I look forward to seeing the takeouts and outcomes of the research.

Sometimes people ask me why I choose to fight the trolls on social media. Why take them on when I could either ignore them or leave the platform? But I've done nothing wrong – why should I be the one forced out of the space I enjoy so much most of the time? And why let these trolls control the narrative, say these terrible things freely without being held to account? I want to reclaim my story by calling them out and ensuring users can see that these people don't have the power to silence me – and nor should they subdue anyone into silence. I know I have the strength to take them on, and that I can do so on behalf of those who might not be comfortable with this kind of fight. And many people have told me how they support and admire what I'm doing.

Another thing to remember is that public figures and many others need and use social media to help make a living. Sportspeople use it to supplement their income and help to fund their sporting career, and if you have a sponsor or brand name behind you, you really have to be on social media. So it's not even an option for many to get off the platforms because of any nastiness on them, even if they wanted to.

I want to help make a change for the next generation of boys and girls who are now living in a world where social media is a mainstay of our lives, and unfortunately trolling is a part of that. How does this generation deal with horrific insults and devastating suggestions at such a young age? It is a problem that many people are thinking about now, and I hope that in a decade, or much sooner, things will be better because of that. We also need to make sure parents have the information and tools to talk to their children about handling themselves on social media. Of course schools and sporting bodies have a part to play in doing this, too.

To the trolls who are so vicious – please think twice before you write abusive messages. Ask yourself, would you like something like that written to a loved one? How would you feel if you read something terribly cruel aimed at you? You never know what effect your words will have on someone and the headspace they're in when you write those words. Everyone out there is fighting a battle that you know nothing about. Please let us live and work in peace. Please let us be on social media and have our fun on it; keep it a collaborative, uplifting, supportive space. Stop the abuse. Words hurt, they leave scars you can't see, they hurt our heart and soul.

Some thoughts on social media

- Always be kind.
- If you have nothing nice to say, don't say anything at all.
- Don't criticise or judge anyone – let people posting do their thing.
- The younger generation should know that receiving mean comments and abuse is *not* okay; I want them to know their worth and that they should talk to their teachers, parents, friends and/or coaches if they receive abuse or threats online. They can get help.
- We should be supportive on social media to make it a wonderful, happy space where everyone can enjoy posting.

My mantra: Use my platform to share and tell the truth to connect with, inspire and empower others.

7.

HEARTBREAK

Accept what is, let go of what was and have faith in what will be.

Tin and me

Tin Bikic is the kindest person I know. He has a heart of gold. He was there for me through years no one else was, my one constant. He is a calm, centred, funny human being.

I called him my rock, and for good reason.

He was supposed to be my forever person, but at the end of 2021 I found myself in a situation I never thought I'd be in – dealing with our relationship breakdown after nineteen years together.

This break-up led me into one of the hardest times of my life. It still hurts my heart now – I think it always will. I thought long and hard about writing this chapter because our separation was, and still can be, incredibly difficult for me to talk about. But I believe my experience is worthwhile sharing because so many of us go through heartbreak in one way or another. I guess it is part of being human – losing people we love. And I think talking about that, and being able to share our pain with others, is one way to deal with these kinds of losses.

Anyone who has been through a separation, divorce or break-up with their partner knows the horrible mix of feelings. For some they include a sense of failure, of rejection; we can feel lonely, inadequate, angry. And when you have abandonment issues already, like I do, the breaking up of a really significant and long relationship can literally floor you. Almost destroy you. The split with Tin nearly destroyed me.

To understand how important he was to my life, let me explain how and when we met.

We met when we were both twenty years old. Our paths first crossed on the tennis tour in 2003. The year before, I had fled my family and my father's abusive ways. I was in a fragile state. I was trying to get my form back, which had had me at No. 4 in the world only a few months before.

At the same time, I was dealing with my father and mother turning up unannounced to WTA events and to hotels where they'd tracked me down in an attempt to coax me 'back home'. My father would arrive at events while I was playing and the WTA security would make him leave. It was horrible – I felt as though he still had me trapped. So in a way there seemed to be no escape from him.

When I look back at my first meeting with Tin, which was at a tournament hotel in Vienna, it was not love at first sight. But a few months later we reconnected and started dating. He quickly become a true ally in my life as I was trying to piece it together following the separation from my family.

Tin was a great listener. I remember feeling almost instantly comfortable with him – he was so calm and would hear people attentively. I think that's the thing I was most struck by – his respectfulness. His calmness in the chaos of my life, and his kindness.

What I also liked about Tin was that he understood sport. In his late teens he had become a talented sprinter, one who had the potential to go to the Olympics, though that dream was stopped by injury and lack of access to facilities because of tough conditions in Croatia. He had an understanding of what it took to be the best you can be as an athlete – how to deal with the highs and the lows that a sporting career can toss up.

I remember at the 2003 US Open I was having a very difficult time with my family – a lot of the reason being that I was still emotionally and financially distancing myself from them. After my mother arrived at my New York hotel room and demanded I sign over our house in Saddlebrook, Florida, to my father, I called Tin, knowing that speaking to him would calm me down and take my focus off the pressure I was feeling. I was really sad.

I lost in the second round of that grand slam and Tin was the first one to call me after the match. I told him I wasn't feeling good; we talked about the disappointment I felt about my tennis, how life was overwhelming. In *Unbreakable* I described how I liked having him to talk to about the day: 'The fact is, right now I really can't be alone. I love talking to someone who actually, I think, understands me. Tin's kindness has won my heart.'

When I go back and read those words, I am struck by how the essence of our relationship, of Tin, barely changed over nineteen years. His daily kindness towards me, a highly traumatised person, was exceptional. Tin embodies a high degree of selflessness, of compassion and care.

We come from polar opposite family backgrounds. His home was full of love and positivity. His family enjoyed each other's company and were wholly supportive of each other's dreams. I was struck early on about how he would often talk about how much he'd learnt from his parents. It's no surprise he embodies the best qualities of them.

As you know by now, I have spent the majority of my life thinking I'm not good enough, but when Tin walked into my life, he willed me to believe in myself. He thought the world of me and he believed in me a lot more than I believed in myself. Also, he implored me to never give up. As our relationship blossomed, more and more he showed me deep loyalty and love. In turn I respected him, leant on him, and adored him, to be frank.

In the years around 2005, when I really hit rock bottom and had become suicidal, Tin was crucial to my recovery. He helped save my life.

I wrote this tribute to him in *Unbreakable*:

Tin, my rock ... We've been together since we were twenty ... He's been an unwavering force by my side through more bad times than good. He has never altered.

Never let me down. Over the years we have been together I have been overweight, depressed, bankrupt and on the verge of ending my life and he has never once said, 'This is too hard, I am leaving.' He accepts me for who I am. He's my best friend and the love of my life.

I would not be where I am today, doing what I do in my career after tennis, had it not been for him backing me and believing in me as much as he did.

Separation

So, in 2021 how did it all fall apart?

We didn't fight. There was nothing rocky about our relationship. If you had been in our company you would have seen we were best friends. Tin was loyal to a fault. We were a great little team. We bounced off each other. He always had my back.

He had gone home to see his father in Zagreb on the eve of the Melbourne lockdown in July 2021. There was nothing unusual about it, he said he would be coming back, we had plans together, and there were no signs to suspect a break-up was coming. He had to visit his father because for so long COVID had stopped us travelling and they hadn't seen each other for more than two years.

I rolled on through the 2021 lockdown in Melbourne alone. The days were long, awful at times and I suffered for it. I spent many, many hours by myself. I would be in communication with Tin on the phone but nothing is a substitute for the physical presence of someone else.

I didn't see the break-up coming. But in early October 2021 I started to sense a slight change in Tin's demeanour. He was a little bit different. How would I describe that? He was a bit distant. He was quieter and also sad.

In Croatia his dad was still dealing with the grief of losing Slava, his wife and Tin's mother. Tin too was still dealing with this loss – he was in deep mourning. I completely understood the importance of him spending time with his family and healing.

But I knew he had not booked a return ticket.

He said he would be back in November. Then he told me he would be back in Melbourne at the end of December. But as the end of December was creeping closer, he wouldn't commit to a return date.

He's an introverted character, a quieter style of person, so it wasn't unusual for him not to be very communicative about what he was doing or planning. But I had a sense something was wrong. Yet in the same breath I didn't know what. He just wasn't quite the same. But I thought whatever was going on with him, we could sort it out like we always did.

Then came a FaceTime call two days before Christmas. It had now been five months of uncertainty about what day he would return but he was still promising he *would* return. So when he called me that day, I was confused: 'It's two days before Christmas and it seems like you have no plans to come back to Melbourne. What is going on?'

Tin started to cry, so much so that it was really hard for him to talk – he was crying a *lot*. I'd barely ever seen him cry in nineteen years – only when he found out his mum was sick, and when she died. And I could see he couldn't quite even say the words, and feeling sick it dawned on me what those words were. But I found the courage to ask, 'Look, are we done here? Are you ever coming back?'

Then he kind of nodded, as in: 'We are done.'

As I held the phone I was plunged into a state of disbelief. *We were over?* It was quite incomprehensible. I was in shock. We had hopes of having children. But then, over the phone, two days before Christmas, he was telling me we were done. My mind went into freefall. It all felt so surreal. Weird. Wrong.

Tin had helped keep me alive over the years when all felt lost. I loved him so much. And I was very proud of what we had built through a great many highs and lows. My relationship with him had been the one and only consistent, constant presence in my life and I thought we would always be there for one another.

The other thing that was hard to stomach was that there had been no blazing fights in our relationship. This combined with Tin's inability to articulate why we were 'done', giving me no reasons before Christmas 2021, left me emotionally scrambling.

I think the most natural first step for any of us when we're faced with devastating news like this is initially to begin to process the shock, but also to immediately try to figure out, why?

So I would spend long hours on the phone to friends trying to process how we had come to this. Of course, I blamed myself. What had I done wrong?

While everyone else in Melbourne seemed to be preparing to spend Christmas with their families, rushing around the city shopping at the last minute, anticipating this big day of the year, which is all about family, loved ones, community, I spent those days attempting to comprehend what had happened to make me alone. At that point, I felt numb.

Christmas Day came. It was the first time I had ever spent it alone. Although friends had invited me into their homes, I just needed to be by myself. I was numb but also shattered. I couldn't imagine being with others, putting on a brave face and pretending to celebrate anything.

It was a hard day. I pushed through it. It's only one day, and it wasn't as if I had lots of happy memories of family Christmases in my childhood. But it was hard recalling the Christmases that Tin and I had spent together – so many in the past two decades, sometimes in Melbourne but often back with Tin's parents.

Carrying on

However, the challenge of Christmas wasn't as big as the challenge I was about to face: working while coping with a highly traumatic event. Six days after our break-up I had to start commentating again. The tennis season was about to hit full swing; there were the usual lead-up events to the Australian Open – because of COVID restrictions we did two tournaments in

Adelaide rather than bouncing around capital cities as usual. I was required to be in the commentary box through these tournaments with my head fully around the day's play and the players on court.

Because you're always live on air, commentating tennis matches is not a job where you can just clock on and off, or simply go through the motions. It requires focus and energy at all times, lots of preparation in the form of research, and really being present. And I was. As I wrote in *Unbreakable*: 'I am a survivor and I will always find a way.' So in the last days of December, despite the pain I was in, I put my head down and got to work.

And when January came, and the first tournament in Adelaide began, I focused on the matches and on my on-court interviews. I was able to smile and act as though nothing was wrong, when inside everything was wrong. I would commentate for hours without a hint my life had fallen apart.

As tough as it was to have this going on in my private life, in a way working helped me to take my mind off what had happened, and being with my colleagues, other commentators, players I knew and the crew from Tennis Australia and Channel 9 was amazing. At the same time, I did have to compartmentalise each day.

Being able to compartmentalise was a skill I learnt as a kid. When my world was melting down around me, on the court I would still be able to perform at my best. I was doing the same thing now, years on, in the commentary booth. Trying to forget my emotional turmoil and concentrate on my work.

Putting on a brave face in those early weeks of 2022 in some ways helped me. My work got me out of the house. I was professional and I stayed good at compartmentalising. But at that time, I thought Tin may come back. And he did give me some hope he would be coming back. He wasn't unequivocal in our conversations that we would never be together again.

Aftermath

As I pushed through every minute of every day, I knew deep down that a crash had to come. The hurt was too much for it not to. You can't sugarcoat healing from something like this as a calm, peaceful experience. It's messy and difficult. It's not pretty.

I sought help from a psychiatrist.

In those sessions I tried to process the break-up. As I've said, I assumed all of it was my fault. This reaction was a product of my childhood, when I was led to think everything was my fault.

I was carrying a massive emotional burden that I had broken the relationship. That Tin just wanted to get away from me. A lot of my past came back because of this. My family blamed me for the breakdown of our family unit, so now I thought I had created this relationship breakdown. All that was haunting me.

My psychiatrist made me see that it was really important *not* to blame myself; that these things happen, sometimes it's impossible to know the reasons, and just because something has broken down, it doesn't mean it's my fault.

Then there was the whole abandonment issue.

I had been abandoned before. It was happening again. On loop in my head was this thought: is there anyone who is going to stick around? And, now, will I be alone forever?

As you know, this break-up led me to a very dark place in April 2022. Recovery in any form would take months and months of therapy, and through those intensive sessions I would finally wake up to the fact of my self-hate, to the extent that it had shaped me and my reactions to life events – good and dreadful, as the split with Tin was. I would understand that my self-worth was in pieces. I was reminded that I had bad PTSD caused by my childhood trauma. It would emerge that I have traits of borderline personality disorder, which contribute to my self-hate and my self-sabotaging in different areas of my life, as well as a great fear of being alone.

So while the break-up has been hard, it has led to other discoveries, which has been good because I have thought for a while that the level of anxiety I'd got used to living with must be extreme. Stuff like being ashamed to look in the mirror. Reactions like that felt like more than just having low self-confidence.

Recovery from a life shock such as a break-up isn't a quick process. If, like I was, you're living with your partner, getting used to living by yourself is a huge adjustment. All the parts of that. Before, it was Tin who cooked every night for us. I have had to get used to living alone – I'd never done it before now.

Holidays are another touchpoint. You're used to automatically having your partner as your holiday companion. Once they're gone, there's a whole new challenge. Who do I go away with? As was the case when I went back to Croatia in 2022, it can be refreshing to take a break alone, but it can also be a really confronting idea.

And then there are the normal parts of life – weekends, public holidays, birthdays, Valentine's Day. All reminders that you're not with someone and everyone else seems to be. If you dread these days and times, believe me, I sympathise.

When I was trying to recover, in the hardest periods in 2022, unquestionably talking to my therapist helped me to reach some healthier conclusions about what was happening than I ever would have been able to get to on my own. I also wrote down advice to myself which I tried to follow. And I found a great list on the Headspace website, which I've put in the Resources section at the back of this book.

Help is the last word

Ultimately, what I know for myself to be true is that getting help was crucial for me in hard times like these. If possible, professional help. At the least, it is good to talk to friends, to read books with advice and understanding about how to recover from heartbreak. Others' understanding is a great help to feeling a bit better.

In late 2022, I was finishing up at a speaking event, about to leave, when a guy came running up to me. 'Oh my gosh, I'm so glad to have heard you speak,' he said. 'I'm a huge fan of yours, I heard you were doing an event, so I didn't want to miss it. I hope you don't mind me coming up to you like this.'

I told him that of course I didn't, and he went on to tell me that when I'd posted on Instagram about the depths of my despair after splitting with Tin, he had read my post and, he said, 'It pushed me to actually go get professional help because I was really struggling and I was on the edge. That post, and you referring to getting professional help, changed my life. I went and got help. It saved me.'

Tin saved my life. His care and support gave me reason to live. I only hope I can do the same for others in their hardest times.

Some things I have learnt from my break-up

- Sometimes heartbreak can't be explained but can be accepted.
- Thoughts I had when the break-up first happened, which I'd say are good to avoid: I blamed myself, was terrified of being alone, was terrified of not finding a relationship like ours again, and fixated on the past and all the memories.
- Things you could do instead: let go and try to accept the situation – this will speed up your recovery; remember you will be smarter because of all the mistakes and experiences whenever you go into your next relationship; know you are a lot stronger than you think you are.
- Regardless of what happens, even if someone has hurt you really badly, it's important to stay kind and live with grace. Try to steer clear of hate, resentment and bitterness.

_____

Mantra: You will not always get closure after a heartbreak, but time can help you move on and create it yourself.

_____

8.

COMMENTARY

*When I was starting over again in my career I had
so much fear, but I know now that getting outside
of your comfort zone can take you to amazing
new heights.*

In 2011, three years before I retired from tennis, I was invited
into the TV broadcast box at Wimbledon to try something I
had wanted to do for a while: commentate.

I became intrigued by tennis commentary midway through
my career. I had always been interested in the way matches
were called and how analysts spoke about tactics and the tech-
nical side of the game. All of that had for some time appealed
to me. And, honestly, even despite my lack of confidence in
most ways, I always felt I'd been able to get into the nitty-gritty
of on-court analysis – even if it was just in my own head or
discussing it with coaches. As a player I liked breaking down
the game, I was interested in how to utilise certain strategies,

and knowing my opponent's strengths and weaknesses, as well as my own.

In 2011 I was ranked 59th in the world going into Wimbledon. I lost in the first round to former French Open champion Francesca Schiavone, which was a tough draw. But it meant I had a bit of time on my hands.

Australian tennis great John Newcombe was commentating at Wimbledon for Channel 7. 'Newk' was a very experienced commentator. (This was the man who had been world No. 1 in both singles and doubles, and in the majors had won seven singles titles, seventeen men's doubles, and two mixed doubles titles.)

So in the middle of the tournament, in a small Wimbledon commentary booth, I took my place beside Newk, and to be honest, I felt at home. Sure, I was nervous, and I didn't really know what I was doing, but I knew I loved talking about tennis. For years I had spent hours analysing my own matches, my opponents' matches. Now here at Wimbledon in 2011 I was getting the chance to have a go at something new.

It was a total thrill.

The match I commentated with Newk featured Serena Williams, arguably the greatest woman tennis player ever, against Australian Jarmila Gajdosova on Wimbledon's Court 1. I spoke about the reason Williams was choosing a certain shot and where she was hitting, or where she was serving and why. It felt natural.

I was in the commentary box for about an hour, and that hour gave me a glimpse of a world I wanted to be part of. The thrill of live television, an opportunity to talk about the game I loved – there was so much I enjoyed about dipping my toe into the commentary world.

Starting out

When I retired in 2014, I was pretty sure I wanted to become a commentator, but I also knew that making it happen would be a challenge. Besides needing a deep knowledge of the game, you have to be able to explain a match and do so in a way the audience will understand. Sure, I was a former world No. 4, but that didn't automatically mean I would be a great commentator.

There were also many hoops to jump through in order to get into this highly competitive world of the media. There was no way I could just walk into a role.

To be honest, at that point I was at a loss about how to break into the world of tennis commentary. I'm not going to lie, I was also afraid. It was natural that I had fear and apprehension. After having just one skill-set for all my life, trying something new was a huge step. Being a tennis player was my identity and I didn't know if I would be good at anything else. It was one thing to have loved my sixty minutes in the booth a few years before; it was a completely different thing to develop the skills required to not only commentate but to commentate well. I had a lot of doubt in my mind: was I being unrealistic to even think I might be able to do it? Was I bound to embarrass myself in trying?

I kept coming back to something one of my coaches had once said to me. I couldn't get it out of my head. He had said to me that I should make sure I played tennis for as long as possible, because I wouldn't be good at anything else. He told me that it was all I knew how to do. I wouldn't be capable of anything else. Maybe, he said, I could go and work in a bakery or something, but that was about it.

So, my self-doubt, and memories of words like these and of my father's verbal abuse, ate away at me. But despite all that, I knew that if I wanted to make something of myself post-tennis, I had to get out of my comfort zone; I had to forget about all the bad comments and believe in myself. And with whatever I did, I was going to have to start from ground zero.

Fortunately, I also had someone important in my corner: Todd Woodbridge. He was the person who had sat me down soon after I retired and willed me to come up with a plan for my life. Todd was instrumental in encouraging me to write my first book, to do some coaching but also he has been the most important person to encourage me to carve out a commentary career. He was key in helping me reinvent myself. He really believed that I could do so many things. The exact opposite of that coach. I'm so grateful to Todd for that belief.

Todd gave me the sage advice early on. First, he told me to say yes to everything – whatever it related to – because it would give me an opportunity to keep on improving and evolving. He taught me to say yes to the smallest of jobs. 'Accept every little thing, it goes on your CV, it's good practice and you will get better from it.'

He helped me to understand what commentating was about, and to practise: early on, after I'd commentated a match, we'd sit down and watch or listen back, either together or I'd do it on my own. Then I could see what was working or where I could take a different approach, for example, if I faltered, or repeated myself, or didn't provide enough insight at a certain point in the match.

He taught me early that it's important to keep pushing, too. That is, pushing through self-doubt, and not being afraid to try new things, in an attempt to find out what I like and what I am good at. Again, it's all about taking every offer, no matter how big or small.

My first forays into commentary were hard. Early on I got a couple of no's from broadcasters. Doors were shut on me. But I kept persisting. I knew there was no job on a platter and that it would take hard work, patience and persistence to get producers to take a chance on me.

So I kept stepping outside of my comfort zone and I kept pushing for an opportunity.

One door that did open was that of Fox Sports. In January 2018, for a couple of minutes of each day at the Australian Open, I did a quick live cross to the Fox Sports host when he was wrapping up the play. With the host I would break down the matches of the day. It was just a few minutes, but the experience in front of the camera was invaluable. I was a little bit nervous at first because of it being live but quite quickly I felt comfortable.

I learnt to speak in concise and informative sentences. I got more practice being under pressure and delivering information sharply and succinctly to a live audience. I found it very different at first – not being on the court felt completely different. But what I found straight away was the love I felt for talking about tennis and still being around it.

And like Todd had advised me to do, I took every opportunity that came my way. At this Australian Open in 2018, I was doing the previews and wrap-ups of each day's play for Fox Sports, some commentary for Tennis Australia and also I woke every morning at 5.30 to do a radio cross about each day's play, which was enjoyable. I wanted so much to get better at this kind of media work so I would be at the courts all day from early morning to late at night, even just to get a sixty-second opportunity: you have to be there on-site to get your chance. You never know what's going to happen on the day so if you're not around you'll miss out on the little things that sometimes pop up.

In 2019 I got to call a couple of matches with Channel 7, and that year I was doing all the previews and wrap-ups with Fox every morning and night. I was also asked to commentate the Australian Open qualifying matches and the main draw for an internal media stream, the Tennis Australia host broadcast. I was speaking in front of a big national audience so it was a good way for me to hone my analysis.

I was of course on a huge learning curve. I made mistakes. I got constructive criticism from colleagues like Todd. That was helpful, and I took everything on and kept trying to get better.

I think when you are starting something new, it's important to accept that you will make mistakes; that mistakes can actually make you better. It's important to be able to take constructive criticism, and be open to feedback – not to be offended by it. I vowed to myself to keep moving forward no matter what the feedback was. I kept telling myself, 'Even if I fail, at least I have tried.' Learning can be hard but I would always give 150 per cent to grow and get better. You have to trust the process. On the tennis court I'd learnt first-hand the benefits of working hard, and in turn I took that work ethic to the commentary booth.

And the better I got, the better the opportunities that came my way.

Big break

At the Australian Open in 2020 I was given a huge shot with Channel 9. In the lead-up to the tournament, Nine put out an announcement about their 'all-star line-up of commentators and hosts'. The channel had gained the rights to broadcast the Open in a six-year contract with Tennis Australia and it was billing itself as 'the new home of tennis'.

The team I'd be commentating alongside included John McEnroe, who I had always respected and whose commentary is renowned as being some of the best and most outspoken in the tennis world. Todd was on the team, as was the seasoned AO commentator Jim Courier.

When Channel 9 announced the team, they wrote of me:

At the age of 16, Jelena Dokic caused one of the biggest upsets in tennis history by beating world No. 1 Martina Hingis at Wimbledon. By the time she was 19, Dokic was ranked No. 4 in the world. She has also penned the best-selling autobiography *Unbreakable*, a book which details her career and well-documented family life.

I was beyond excited to be working with these legends. The two people I most admire in the commentary world, and outside of it, are Todd and Jim. Both are inspirational to me not only as players but also in what they've since achieved. While I was still playing and they were already in their commentary roles, I used to listen to them because I loved their insights. Todd even called a few of my matches back in the day.

Jim has been one of the best commentators around for years. To this day, not that he knows this, I still get incredibly nervous taking up the seat beside him in the booth. It's partly because I remember him while I was playing, how much I loved his commentary, and I looked up to him when I started thinking about my second career.

It's the same thing with Todd. He's a really good friend, and he's also one of the best all-round commentators, hosts and interviewers in the world. I've always been inspired by him and how he reinvented himself after retiring from tennis; how well he's done in the media world. Even to this day, I'm not sure where I would be without his calm, considered, thoughtful career counsel. He was the first person I went to for advice after

I retired in 2014 and he remains the person I seek out today when it comes to commentary and career. He has shown an extraordinary amount of care and dedication in ensuring I am the best person I can be, both in and out of the commentary box. Todd didn't have to give up hours of his time to ensure I could push forward in this world, but he did. Most of all he believed in me and for that I will be eternally thankful.

I put in an enormous amount of preparation to make sure I could stand proud alongside my team in 2020. Every morning I took pages and pages of notes on the players in the matches I'd be calling. I did research online. I listened to other commentators. I pored over the information that producers at Channel 9 provided, things like statistics and players' backgrounds. I did a whole lot of research about every single player and how they matched up with opponents.

I always overprepare. You might feel like you need three facts or figures or insights from past matches but you have six. Because you never know what is coming, especially with on-court interviews. You have to be ready for any kind of answer or situation.

With commentary, I like to go into the mind of the player; a place I know well. This is one of the main things I try to bring to the table; I know what it is like being a player. That said, no matter how much you think you understand the sport, commentating is a completely different experience. It's not just about knowing the game; you have to learn the nuances of a match and then be able to explain them clearly to viewers. You want to communicate the feeling of a match to the audience. And it can be interesting to talk about how the players might be feeling at a particularly important moment by thinking back to those key, tense moments in your own career.

You have to be careful to express yourself clearly; know how to modulate your voice (when to go up and down); when to say more before or after a point, and when it's best to let the play sink in for the audience and not over-commentate, which can be annoying for viewers. You have to be very articulate.

During 2019 I began to absolutely love being on live TV. The feeling of adrenalin was very much like being on a tennis court and taking on an opponent in front of an attentive audience. This aspect of it all I was really comfortable with. I loved the pressure.

Succeeding

My persistence, resilience and hard work rewarded me with a multi-year contract with Channel 9 to commentate all four grand slam majors from the start of 2021.

I started to relax into my role and I was provided with some incredible opportunities. One of them was to do on-court interviews at the 2021 Australian Open.

An interview I loved doing was one with the incredible Serena. I thought back to my first-ever commentating experience, watching Serena play at Wimbledon a whole decade earlier. If someone had told me then that ten years on I'd be talking with her after she had won her fourth-round match at the Australian Open, I would have laughed at them! And yet here she was, having just beaten Aryna Sabalenka.

Serena and I played each other four times over my career. She is an awe-inspiring player and person. As I stood interviewing her in 2021, I felt extremely nervous. I hadn't slept very well the night before, even though I am pretty good at performing under pressure. I knew I had time for about four questions to ask but I had ten ready. My main focus was to try to have a nice chat.

As soon as the interview started, I relaxed a bit – partly because Serena was very kind. She smiled at me just after my first question and that made it all easier. The interview went really well, I think because of that.

I started warmly:

It's so good to see you again. We used to share a court together. Haven't seen you in a while; now we're sharing the court again. You're still doing your thing and winning, I'm in a little bit of a different capacity in a different role and I'm just hoping you'll be a little bit less brutal than when I played you because I'm still a bit nervous to interview you.

The crowd laughed, I could hear them, and Serena seemed to be enjoying herself too – she laughed and was lovely.

Williams: 'We've had some formidable matches.'

Me: 'A couple, but I think they were a little bit more enjoyable for you than they were for me.'

She was fantastic to interview, she ran with my questions, and when I decided to go off the subject of tennis, to give the crowd something different, we talked about her fabulous catsuit outfit, which was bright pink and red, shot through with black. I asked her where the idea for it had come from and she told me it was inspired by US sprinter Flo-Jo. We talked about her gorgeous three-year-old daughter, who was learning tennis, and I was thrilled when Serena congratulated me on my questions after I asked her about her art collection.

I felt as though all my preparation the night before had been worth it when she told me how she loved what I was asking her. I felt we had a great rapport out there and had a lot of fun.

One of the interviews that moved me the most was with Frenchwoman Alize Cornet. Cornet had triumphantly finally made a grand slam quarter-final at the 2022 Australian Open, after an incredible sixty-three attempts. I was so happy for her. She and I had practised many times during my career and we got on well (though we never played a competitive match against each other). She was always very friendly towards me. So that blazing summer's day in 2022 I was thrilled to witness her win. As a fellow player who'd endured many ups and downs on the circuit, I could imagine how emotional she must be feeling, beating Romanian Simona Halep, so I started the interview by embracing her. Then we talked:

Me: I'll do a little bit first, because I know how much this means to you. That's why I went to hug you. I know how emotional it is. Here in 2009, you were in the fourth round.

Cornet: Yes.

Me: That was thirteen years ago. I was waiting to play also my match in the fourth round, to play the winner of you and [Dinara] Safina in the quarter-finals. You had a couple of match points. I know how hard that was for you. I can see how emotional you are. It means so much to you. This is your first ever grand slam quarter-final.

When I said this, the crowd cheered and applauded, and it gave me goosebumps. I asked Cornet what was going through her head.

Cornet: It feels amazing. The battle that we had with Simona today with this heat and after thirty minutes of game, we were both dying on the court and we kept going for two and a half hours, with all our hearts. Congrats to Simona . . . She's such a fighter and she's an example for me and to beat her today, to go to my first quarter-final, it's just a dream come true. I don't know what to say, it's just magic.

Me: Amazing . . . I'm so happy for you, we all are. Congratulations. Your first grand slam quarter-final.

Cornet: Thank you.

Then, just as I was wrapping up, Alize interjected: 'Wait, wait,' she said. 'So I just want to thank my box first, but also I want to tell you something, how you moved on in your life, I think we can all congratulate you. You were an amazing player and now an amazing commentator.'

As I stood on Rod Laver Arena, I felt tears forming in the corners of my eyes. 'You just made me cry. I can't believe I'm crying. Thank you, Alize Cornet.'

Afterwards, under the stadium stands, I was still wiping tears from my eyes. I was so moved. The act of kindness from Alize, praising me for piecing my life back together and for now having a great career, was unbelievably selfless from her in the biggest moment of her career. I will never forget it.

My other favourite interview was on Rod Laver Arena at the Australian Open in 2023, when I interviewed world No. 1 Novak Djokovic. The Serbian-born star and I have traced a similar geographical childhood path, growing up in war-torn Yugoslavia, but we really hadn't seen each other properly in a couple of years. And now we were meeting on Rod Laver Arena on live television as he had just beaten Bulgarian player Grigor Dimitrov in the third round.

'It's nice to see you, Jelena, I haven't seen you in ages,' was the first thing Novak said to me. When I asked him about the first time we'd met each other at the Australian Open back in the day, he correctly said that we had spoken in 2006 – two years before he won the tournament for the first time, and four years after we had our first practice session together.

It led to a very funny exchange on Centre Court as the cameras rolled.

'You came to me in 2006, and you said, "Hi, I'm Novak Djokovic – do you remember me?"' I reminded Novak. 'And I said to you, "Yes I do," and I have to admit, I didn't. We hit two years earlier – I pretended I did, but . . . I definitely know who you are now!'

That brought laughter and cheers from the crowd, and Novak, as did what Djokovic said next: 'Well, to return the compliment to you, I was looking up to you, obviously. You played for Australia but you came from our region, we speak the same language and you were a big star at the time. I was really happy to play with you, it's great to see you again.'

'The pleasure is all mine,' I replied, smiling.

To interview one of the greatest players of all time is such a privilege, especially on Rod Laver Arena, my home and my home grand slam, and I will be forever grateful for this interview, and for Novak's generosity and the time he gave me. He really made my job a lot easier – it felt like two friends talking and he enabled that because he was so engaging. Novak is someone who, from the beginning, going back seventeen years to when I first met him, has always been warm to me, always stops to have a chat and a catch-up, is generous with his time. Most people don't see this side of him and that he's truly a great person.

I get a lot of joy out of candid moments like this, and being able to bring my knowledge into these interviews. After interviewing Novak, I had the same thrill and sense of awe as after Serena and I had chatted on court: if someone had told me, even five years back, when I had no idea whether I would make it in this world, that I would be interviewing tennis greats like her and Novak, who I have so much respect for, I'd have said, 'No frickin way will that happen.'

Always learning

Five years into my media career, what I know to be true is that hard work, preparation, patience, discipline and continuing to grow your knowledge are powerful tools, not just for a commentator but in any profession.

Another thing I know is that you always have to be on. Despite the fatigue you may feel in the second week of a grand slam tournament, you have to erase tiredness from your voice. You have to exude energy in the commentary box. You have to keep pushing. I actually don't mind that – I like to push myself to the limit, to see how much I can do. You have to give a lot of yourself in commentary and on live TV, and while you're doing that often you're not going to feel 100 per cent. So it's all about how you perform when you don't feel your best. Just like as a tennis player. At the end of a big day I feel tired but satisfied – I call it 'grateful tired'.

The hours are long during a grand slam. During the Australian Open I am usually at Melbourne Park from dawn to dusk and a lot of times well into the night. You might find me on the *Today* show at the crack of dawn, and then on a panel as the day starts. Then I'll commentate a couple of matches through the day, do some news crosses going into the evening, and then the night session begins. Us commentators have been known to find a couch to snooze on between matches and appearances. And by the time the grand slam is over I find myself sleeping for days, exhausted and feeling that grateful tired. I never forget how lucky I am to do this job. And I wouldn't have it any other way. It's so great being at Melbourne Park doing what I love in a sport that I have so much passion for, spending time with colleagues and friends, grabbing a coffee with them if there is a spare moment. I enjoy the arduous and intense nature of it all. I can say now, with absolute certainty, I love commentating and TV as much as I loved playing tennis.

This is quite the revelation for me. I didn't think I would find anything that would fill that gap that tennis left in my life. Around the time *Unbreakable* came out, I was completing a coaching qualification with Tennis Australia. I wanted to take the course to broaden my chances when it came to starting over in a new career. It was another skill to have, I figured, and perhaps it would help to fill that gap. I really enjoyed the work – I ended up coaching different age groups, men and women, recreational players, competitive juniors, kids. The work gave me a chance to improve my communication skills, and to support people in doing something we both loved. I kept it up until pretty recently but eventually my commentary and public speaking had to take precedence. But I'm so pleased I did it and I would really recommend learning new skills and if possible getting new qualifications to keep learning and broadening your opportunities.

Being able to commentate and analyse tennis for a job is a total honour. I feel so fortunate to have found my calling (pardon the pun) and will do everything in my willpower to keep getting better.

During a tournament and always in my general life I sub-scribe to the belief 'win the morning, win the day'. By this I mean that I believe waking up early always pays off as it's extra time for research and preparation. Also, it's a great feeling to know I've achieved something while most people are still asleep: there's something powerful in knowing that the day is only just starting for many, but I've already done a good chunk of work, or had some quiet time. That's why, when I was a tennis player, I'd regularly practise early in the morning. I was brought up like this and learnt it from coaches, as well as from the first people on tour who embraced early-morning practice: Monica Seles, Steffi Graf and Serena and Venus Williams. Venus and Serena used to play night matches all the time, especially at grand slams, but when I would be going for my early practice at 7 a.m. the next day, they would also be there, back on court, dedicated to their training.

It is powerful and empowering knowing that you have already worked hard while others are sleeping. You know what they say: 'The early bird catches the worm.'

Public speaking

During my book tour in 2017, I started to feel more comfortable speaking in front of big audiences. A few people suggested to me that I should think about taking my story on to the speaking circuit, shaping it into something like a motivational talk. At that point I was beginning to realise that sharing what I had been through with others could help people in lots of different ways, so this idea appealed to me.

I worked hard to come up with a forty-minute presentation. As I always do, I threw myself into getting prepared. I got professional input about how my speech would read, and hired a speaking coach to help me to communicate my words in the most compelling and engaged ways. I found this work very fulfilling and by the time I was ready to launch myself on to the circuit, I was ready and I had a great keynote presentation for clients and audiences.

_____

Sharing my story continues to heal me and I feel gives hope to others.

_____

Like I can in writing my books, in my speaking work I can raise awareness of serious issues. I give so much of myself in my keynote presentations. And I always do a Q&A session after them because I love to give people a chance to participate and ask me about topics they're curious about. I also just love connecting with the audience. I meet so many people now I'm on the speaking circuit full-time, and being able to meet those who come to my talks, as well as people from all sorts of different companies and brands, foundations, charities, schools and different sports, is incredibly rewarding.

If someone had told me when I retired nearly a decade ago that I would be a motivational speaker, an author of a bestselling book, that I would also be dipping my toes into co-hosting on TV on top of my media career, I would have said they were crazy. But we are capable of so much more than we think we are. My life is testament to that – and so are many others. My speaking is something I love just as much as my TV work and it's shown me that if you open yourself up to new experiences and new directions, you never know what's around the corner. And if you decide to embark on a new career, or take up something you've never tried, you have to believe that eventually you'll nail it and it will have always been the right choice. Because really that's what life is all about – learning new things, self-education. Even if you don't always succeed, it's never a failure, it's a lesson, especially if you have given it 100 per cent. Trust your capabilities and don't let others tell you that you can't do something. Where would I have been if I'd listened to everyone who didn't believe in me, including that coach who doubted what I could achieve.

The first step

My advice for people who are thinking of changing careers, or of transforming their life in some way, or, if you're just starting out in a new area, is that the hardest thing is taking the first step – but be brave and do everything in your power to fight that fear. Take a leap of faith! And back yourself.

- Be persistent, ask, and ask again for what you want.
- Don't say no to any opportunity – no matter how small.
- Fear is natural. But being willing to take the risks and being brave will help you push through that wall.
- It's not about being perfect – you will make mistakes and that's normal. Mistakes are lessons that make you better.
- Take constructive criticism in a positive way – to improve.

- Change can be scary but what is scarier is allowing fear to stop us from growing, improving, evolving and being better and wiser.
- I really believe in hard work. It always pays off: what you put in is what you'll get out.
- Be patient – progressing in a career can take a long time; you've got to take it a step at a time. Trust the process, keep focused.
- Be really open and excited about learning new things, but take time to master each one.
- Don't give up or quit at the first hurdle. Get comfortable with being uncomfortable. If you are not failing and making mistakes, you are not learning and improving.

Five things I believe you need no matter what you are trying to achieve

- Hard work – to improve and have success you need to be prepared, and learn from failures and losses. Always hustle. Educate yourself to the max.
- Motivation – it's never too late to set another goal or dream.
- Perseverance – always continue despite the failures, losses and difficulties. Remember, perseverance is falling down twenty times but getting up twenty-one. It is extremely hard to beat a person who never gives up.

- Resilience – it's how you react in the face of adversity. It's the capacity and ability to maintain strength and purpose in the toughest of circumstances and the ability to always keep going.
- Courage – it's okay to be afraid; fear is a part of life but we get through things by being courageous, taking risks, and going for it.

Mantra: Say yes to all opportunities! Work hard. Believe in yourself and don't give up on your dreams.

9.

BELIEF

'Faith consists in believing when it is beyond the power of reason to believe.'
Voltaire

For too long I felt unworthy of love. I had zero self-belief, was sure that I wasn't enough, especially in the eyes of my father. But at the end of 2003 a woman stepped into my life who was able to take up a parental role; a woman who was a consistent presence and showed me a type of love I had never experienced: unconditional love.

Unconditional love

Slava Bikic was the mother of Tin and was one of the few people I have met who has truly welcomed me into her world and cared for me as a parent would. She gave me an insight on how parents should love.

The year 2003 was another difficult one. My tennis was becoming more and more erratic as my mental capacity diminished every day. My father was furious that I had got together with Tin. Repeatedly, he'd threatened to kill my boyfriend. The problem wasn't just that I had a relationship; a lot of it was that my father didn't approve of Tin because he was Croatian and Catholic, whereas my father identified the family as Serbian Orthodox. For my father this was the biggest betrayal and a good reason to hate my new partner, and to spread that hate. I am really supportive of every race and religion and my father's stand on this sickened me. I worried for a while that all the pressure might make Tin walk away – because of my father hounding us about him being the 'wrong' religion, and him throwing so many vile threats around.

But while my father was his usual destructive self, Tin's family was nothing but supportive of me from the moment I met them.

In 2003 Tin and I travelled to the city of Zagreb so I could meet his parents for the first time. I remember being nervous and worried about what they'd think of me. But Slava and Borna Snr, Tin's dad, immediately made me feel welcome.

Slava had beautiful thick dark hair and kept a cosy, warm, welcoming household, where family meals were times for celebration and lively conversation. It all seemed so perfect – hard for me to believe. Straight away it was clear this was an extraordinarily different environment from the home I had experienced. The first thing I noticed was the kindness shared between the family, the generosity in the way they talked to each other.

Borna Snr, Tin's dad, was a chemical engineer, and Slava had owned an award-winning sleepwear brand. Sadly they had lost this business during the war. But they were a resilient couple, always positive, and when I met them they were level-headed and hopeful about the future, and about their sons' futures.

Tin's mother had gone through a lot in her life. The hardest loss she'd suffered was one of her brothers dying when she was pregnant with Tin. And Tin's dad had had a tough upbringing – he'd lived on his own from the age of fifteen, and had put himself through school, and then college, in Zagreb. Borna Snr was quiet while his wife was the chattier one – and you could see she also had a quiet strength. She and Borna Snr cooked hearty, delicious food, and when they all came together it was clear she loved her family so much. As I sat there at the Bikic dinner table when I first spent time with the four of them, with everyone calm and having 'regular' conversations about all sorts of things, I could barely focus on the chat, I was so preoccupied, thinking to myself, wow, this is the kind of household that I would like to live in.

A place of consistency, love, support, kindness and warm hearts. A safe place.

The exact opposite of what I grew up with.

Ever since I was a small child I had seen many awful events at dinner time: a table flipped in anger, food thrown in a rage, silent seething across the table, cruel words thrown – all driven by my father. When you live in an abusive home, unpredictable, frightening family dinners become the norm.

I was transported in Tin's household to a whole other world that I had never been part of. To be honest, I was taken aback by it all. It's very hard to understand and know that homes like Tin's exist when you lived with the opposite of that every single day for nearly two decades.

Also overwhelming to me in this moment was the revelation that this was how stable parents showed love. From the age of six I was beaten; from the age of eleven, I'd had it drilled into me, 'You're a cow.' From the age of thirteen it was, 'You're a whore.' Imagine what that does to your self-esteem and confidence. For sure you end up hating yourself, believe you are nothing but useless – that is, until someone like Slava enters your life.

As my relationship with Tin grew stronger by the year, the Bikics frequently welcomed me into their family. And when I was in Slava's company there, the way she spoke to me, spoke about me, gave me such a boost of confidence in myself. She was one of those extremely generous, compassionate people who doesn't think about herself. So giving. She was there when I was feeling flat, when my mental health troubles were overwhelming me, and when I was flying. Always a caring presence, who I consciously began to see as a mother figure in years when my relationship with my own mum was sadly fractured.

Slava and Borna Snr went to church every Sunday and they seemed to derive peace and joy from that, which they passed on to us. What I noticed with Slava was that at first she offered me friendship, and then it turned to love, and she never asked things of me. My father always wanted more and more from me, but whatever I gave him of myself was never good enough. The reverse was true of Slava. And, of course, of Tin, who encouraged me and steadied me for so many years. Borna Snr, too, was extremely loving and supportive of us. Something I loved about him and Slava was that they didn't see me as Jelena Dokic, the tennis player; to them I was simply Jelena. They loved me for me.

Shining a light

In 2008 I had dragged myself out of the pits of despair with the goal of playing at the 2009 Australian Open. I was unranked. By the summer of 2009 I was ranked as No. 187. I was twenty-five years old and in good shape when I entered the Australian Open wild-card play-off and won my way into the 2009 draw.

As you know, through grit and top-class play, I made the quarter-finals, which was almost unthinkable for me. Those weeks were an extraordinary time. I was elated, hopeful. And for once, someone I loved and looked up to insisted Tin and I keep all the newspaper clippings and magazine clippings of my success, of this magical Australian Open run. At the time, I didn't know why. My father either threw out or had sold my trophies, including my Wimbledon medal and my Hopman Cup diamond ball.

When Tin and I returned to Croatia the next time, we gave the press clippings to Slava and she had them framed, then hung them on a wall she had dedicated to my tennis career. Of course, there were also photographs of her sons on the wall, but what I could never get over was the fact she had carved out a space for me, to celebrate me. She was proud of the couple we were, how we looked out for each other, but she was also proud of me alone.

For the first time in so long, I felt people had my back, cared about me, and cared about my successes rather than my failures.

Slava proudly kept a notebook of all my victories on the court, picking up my achievements and shining a light on them as they happened and in the years afterwards. And she would say, 'Jelena, you can do so much. You have the potential to do anything you want, even outside of tennis.'

When she said this to me the first time, I was confused. Me? Something outside of tennis? At that time, I didn't even dare think of a life outside tennis. But Slava made me believe that I was capable of other things in life. That is, I was more than my tennis career. 'You've done so much but you've got the potential to do much more,' she'd say. I would feel this was almost incomprehensible: tennis was all there was, the only thing I was good at, the only thing I knew how to do – it was my world. It was totally foreign, the prospect that I could do anything beyond the sport.

When my TV commentary career started to take off, she was also the first to say, 'I told you, you're so capable. I always believed in you. I am proud that you found something that you love and something you are good at. You just have to believe in yourself.'

Slava was the person who really made me do that – for the first time. I felt a great warm wave of hope when I was around her. That I *was* capable of things. She was, aside from Tin and his dad, a consistently positive presence in my life.

Legacy

On 14 November 2019, our hearts were obliterated when cancer claimed Slava's life. She fought hard and even in her last months, weeks and days, she remained selfless to a fault. She didn't want to be a burden on her family, and although she was eventually in a very sick state, she would consistently ask us about our lives. How were *we* doing? What were *our* plans? What were *our* dreams? Our hopes? What grand slams was I going to commentate next? What she did not want was to talk about herself and whether she was in pain and whether she was struggling. She still had an incredible amount of compassion in that time. She was still selfless, a gracious fighter.

It was terrible to see the cancer taking over her body. You never want to see someone you love in that condition, fighting for their life.

From the day she was diagnosed to the day she died it was eight months. Tin and I felt an enormous amount of grief after she passed. Today, I still wish I could reach out to her and talk to her. I wish I could call her.

I will be eternally grateful for the most important things she gave me: belief, love, lessons, kindness. She came into my life, she made me see the light amid much darkness, because she believed in me. She believed in me so much that I started to believe in myself. She loved me for being me. That is the greatest gift of all. People like Slava come along once in a lifetime.

I will forever be grateful to Slava for accepting me, loving me in the same way she would a daughter, and taking me into her home. She was there in some of the worst times of my life and I will never forget her care. She used to call me her 'sweet one'. That meant a lot to me. I really hope that I gave her as much love and happiness as she gave me. I really hope she knew how much she meant to me.

Rest in peace, Slava.

Love always, Jelena.

I want to share the post I dedicated to her.

Dokic_Jelena

We lost an amazing woman today.

An incredible, kind, loving and selfless woman and MOTHER. To me an amazing mother in law who took me in and cared for me and loved me like her own.

I am struggling to believe that you are gone. We are broken, our hearts are broken.

I will miss our conversations and our laughs. I will miss your wisdom, kindness and pure heart. It's killing me to know that I will never see you again, hug you or get to talk to you ever again.

I will never forget the first time that I met you and how you accepted me into your home and your life with kindness and a smile on your face.

Belief

You always believed in us and had faith in us. Thank you for that and your positivity because it got us through the toughest of times.

You were our strength, our rock and our everything.

You left us too quickly and too early. A huge loss and a hole in our hearts that I am not sure how we will ever fill that hole or recover from this.

Thank you for the support that you gave us and especially to your son and I. We will be grateful for that forever.

Thank you for raising your son and my everything the way that you did. To be such an incredible and kind human being with the purest heart.

We will cherish the memories that we had with you forever. You are gone but never forgotten and always loved.

You are in a better place now, looking down on us and we hope to make you proud.

We love you more than you could ever imagine and thank you for the time that we had with you.

You will always be in our hearts. Forever.

RIP OUR ANGEL.

Till we meet again.

Your son and daughter in law forever, Tin and Jelena.

What if?

I have to admit, I've spent too many hours wondering, if I'd had even one parent to look up to, a parent who loved me, a role model to be inspired by, how would things have gone for me? Would I have had mental health issues if I'd grown up with a mother like Slava, a consistent, firm but warm presence in my life? How would my tennis career, my life, have evolved?

Equally, if I hadn't been with Tin, and had his family around me during the years he and I were together and Slava was alive, I honestly don't know if I would still be here.

And of course if I hadn't had them looking out for me, encouraging me, loving me, then I'd have had only the opinions of my father constantly ringing in a loop round and round in my head.

I know with all my heart that the ways parents and carers look after their kids, the household they create for children in their care, are crucial to a young person's wellbeing. And the facts tell us this. The Australian Institute of Family Studies describes how:

> For some adults, the effects of child abuse and neglect are chronic and debilitating . . . In attempting to explain some of the adverse outcomes associated with chronic . . . maltreatment a concept that is often employed is complex trauma. Complex trauma reflects the . . . broad range of cognitive, affective and behavioural outcomes associated with prolonged trauma, particularly if occurring early in life.

Therapy has shown me that it's very unlikely I'd have the diagnoses I have if I'd had someone like Slava in my life from when I was a baby or a young child. But I know it's futile and bad for my mindset to dwell on the 'what if'. Instead, I want to spread a message of gratitude to women such as Slava and a former coach of mine, Lesley Bowrey, who showed me how to believe in myself, and how I deserve to be treated. (I'll talk more about Lesley later in the book.) They made me see what true love is. They made me see that a home without family abuse exists. They made me realise that success should not have its roots in abuse.

My mum

I love my mum. Today, we are in a good space. But our relationship has been complicated and difficult in the past – especially when I was a teenager and my father's violence was at its worst. This is one of the hardest parts of my life and upbringing to write about – feeling sometimes as though my mother couldn't really be there for me when I was at my most vulnerable.

Then, there was a lot of pain for me because my mother never took my side, never stuck up for me when my father was abusing me and never tried to defend me when he was physically and verbally attacking me. It's taken an immense amount of time for me to reconcile that she felt unable to help me when my father was doing all those terrible things.

My mum was also a victim of her husband, of my father, and so has survived family violence too. I witnessed what happened to her with my own eyes. His dreadful words. His taunts. But when he was abusing me, I wished so hard she was in a place to step in. When the torrents of abuse from my father started, as a young teenager I often wondered why she wouldn't pack up Savo and me and leave. But, even then, wrapped up in that question, I think I understood how hard it would be for us all to escape him. My mother had no money of her own. Also, she desperately wanted Savo and me to be brought up in a family with a father and a mother. The reason why? My mum's mother died when my mum was only fourteen, and her father was killed in a car accident when she was thirteen.

In recent years I have tried hard to understand more deeply where my mum has come from and why she was unable to speak up for me or leave our abusive family home. She loved my father, but she depended on him as well. She depended on him financially, for housing, and she was frightened of his moods, his temper, and his physical abuse. He'd got her into his thrall. She never had any voice in what we did, where we moved to, or lived, but she was the one who had to get work so we had money to buy food and pay rent when we first arrived in Serbia and then Australia. My father was far too busy coaching me.

There's more awareness now about elements of abuse like 'coercive control' – where someone in a relationship introduces controlling and manipulative behaviour which means all the agency is squashed out of the other person. I'm sure that's a lot of what my father imposed on my mum, but I also know that he hit her too. It was not a good situation for her.

When I finally gathered the courage to leave my family in October 2002, aged only nineteen, I left late at night. As I wrote the note to slip under my mum's hotel door, I knew that when she returned home she would bear the brunt of his rage at my fleeing. I wrote that note knowing the pain he was going to inflict upon her, and in it I asked for her forgiveness.

Those days after I left would have been horrible for her. And it didn't take my father long to track me down. He found me at the Porsche Grand Prix, a tennis event being held in Stuttgart, Germany. He arrived there to collect me. To bring me home. Fortunately, WTA officials and security would not let him near me. But he had Savo with him, as a bargaining tool. He would stop at nothing, my father – he used my baby brother to try to get me back under his control. And there were times after I left that my mother was also sent to find me and berate me with a message from him – that I was to come home and it was shameful that I had split from the family unit.

As I mentioned, she was the one my father sent to me before the US Open in 2003 when he wanted me to sign over our house to him. She was really cold to me, angry and distant. She called me some terrible names. At the time, I was extremely hurt and confused by her behaviour, but I also knew that in that moment she blamed me for breaking up the family she had so badly wanted to keep as a unit; that she would do anything to try to keep our nuclear family intact – no matter the effect on me – hoping life would become better.

I used to be filled with anger by all of it – her not defending me, her staying by my father's side, her defending *him*. Even when I was writing *Unbreakable*, years later, I was not in a whole place of forgiveness. The memories of our relationship were still very painful. But I have come to a stage of my life where I have accepted the past for what it is, and tried to understand what she was going through in those years. My mum has said sorry to me, she's shown me remorse for her behaviour in those years. That's a big thing because my father has never done that. It's helped me to move on, to give her another chance and try to build a better relationship with her. We have talked through these times and had some tough conversations. I think we're at a stage where we can have a healthy relationship and I am happy about that.

It was on my holiday to Croatia in 2022 that I felt we had reached the best place we've been in for a long time. We had conversations about the past but also about where we are now.

We had a good week and I'm just glad things are better.

_____

Mantra: The people who believe in us no matter what are the greatest gift. They can be friends if your family can't provide you with unconditional belief and love. Search for the best people in your life and nurture those relationships.

_____

10.

FIGHTING FOR EQUALITY

*Don't dismiss, silence or disrespect women in
any field or any part of everyday life.*

For a very long time, women have been fighting for equal rights. And while the situation is slowly getting better, we are still not at parity. Far from it. Men have a head start on women in lots of different ways. They are likely to be paid more; they don't have to take time off to have children; they are less likely to take time off to be the primary carer of their children; and they are much less likely as adults to be the victim of intimate partner violence. There are still far more men in leadership positions through society than women, and men are less likely to shoulder the burden of domestic duties in heterosexual relationships.

So what about in tennis? Let's start with pay. Nowadays women and men have equal pay at grand slams. In 1973, the

US Open became the first grand slam to offer equal prize money – Billie Jean King had been advocating for this for years and she finally won through. The Australian Open was the next – finally in 2001 they offered both the men's and women's champions the same financial prize. The French Open and then Wimbledon made the change in 2007. Some tour events also offer equal prize money to men and women. That's it, though – the other tournaments have big disparities in the prize money the players receive.

Even to get to this point has taken us decades, and the argument still comes from some male players and men outside of the sporting world that women don't deserve equal pay at grand slams because they don't play the best of five sets, 'only' the best of three. I find this argument incredibly shallow and ignorant. And I don't know what the excuse is in all the other tournaments, where everyone plays the best of three but the women still have lower prize money. Just one case is the Rome Masters 1000: in 2023 the men's champion, Daniil Medvedev, received €1,105,265, and the women's champion, Elena Rybakina, picked up just under half of that: €521,754. We are so far from equity – in 2023!

I want to go back here to speak a bit more about the fight for equal pay that Billie Jean King started in 1970, and in the process how she brought together a group of women we now call the 'Original Nine'. These were nine players who risked their careers to fight for women's rights in tennis.

In 1970 Billie Jean found out that having won Wimbledon in 1968, her prize money was £750 but Rod Laver's – the men's champion that year – was £2000. And not only was the prize money for women far less than for men in all the tournaments at that time, but there were fewer women's events being put on by tennis authorities, which meant fewer opportunities for women to play and to earn prize money.

Billie Jean decided to do something. She set up a totally new tournament in 1970 in Texas called the Houston Women's Invitational. The US Lawn Tennis Association was furious when they found out about this new competition for women only, and threatened to suspend anyone who signed up to play in it. This put off many top women players from participating, but eight refused to be intimidated: Peaches Bartkowicz, Rosie Casals, Julie Heldman, Kristy Pigeon, Nancy Richey, Valerie Ziegenfuss and two Australians, Judy Dalton and Kerry Melville Reid. Along with Billie Jean King, these women signed on to what would become the Virginia Slims Circuit, which in 1973 became the Women's Tennis Association, with Billie Jean as its first president.

One of the Australian players of the nine, Judy Dalton, is still fighting for women's rights at the age of eighty-five, and in January 2023 she and fellow Australian Kerry Melville Reid were joined in Melbourne by six of the other Original Nine to take part in events (delayed because of the pandemic) to commemorate that incredible year of 1970. Dalton told the *Age*: 'Everybody thought that we'd done it because we wanted equal prize money. That wasn't the principle of it. We wanted recognition and to earn enough to be able to make a living. We wanted a door open.'

After the 2023 Australian Open semi-final, won by Elena Rybakina, I interviewed Elena on court and took a minute to pay tribute to the Original Nine: 'I personally want to thank you for everything you have done for tennis and beyond for women and girls,' I said. 'And I speak for everyone when I say thank you. How special is it to play in front of these incredible legends here, and what they have done for women and women's tennis to make it a leading global sport – they risked everything, they risked their careers and they gave us a voice.'

Elena also thanked those seven legends in the audience that night, and all of the Nine, agreeing that their bravery and principles in standing up for their beliefs, making a stand for equality, had had huge and positive repercussions for the new generation of players. I'm so glad we got that chance to personally offer them our respect and regard.

The Original Nine did so much for women's tennis, but it's extraordinary how much sexism and disregard for equality still exist on the circuit today. In May 2023 the Madrid Masters 1000 tournament was forced to issue an apology because it did not allow the women's doubles' champions to address the crowd after their win, having let the men speak to the audience after theirs. As one of the finalists, Jessica Pegula, said, 'I don't know what century everyone was living in when they made that decision.' Victoria Azarenka tweeted, 'Hard to explain to [son] Leo that mommy isn't able to say hello to him at the trophy ceremony.'

The tournament CEO admitted they'd made a mistake and promised, 'This will not ever happen again.' Most people agreed that was too little too late. Earlier in the tournament there'd been controversy over the ball girls' outfits: the ball girls on the main court were in fact models, who'd been dressed in crop tops and short skirts. The actual ball kids were put on the outside courts. For those younger kids, the chance to work on the main court and see their idols playing is a big deal – it inspires their own training and love of the sport. So that was a big miss by the tournament, as well as the sexism it showed parading models on centre court. 'It's a feminised way of treating girls versus guys, who don't dress like that,' Pilar Calvo, spokesperson for the Association for Women in Professional Sport, said. 'In the end, it is a form of sexist violence that is so widespread because people don't even notice it.'

Playing tennis as a woman

Treating women and men equally should be completely unrelated to our physical strength. In tennis, women players work just as hard as men, train as hard, face the same mental challenges on court and the same pressures – those that come from digging deep, match after match, to find the resolve to win. In fact, I would say women face more pressures.

For example, something that's rarely acknowledged are the physical symptoms that women face monthly. We have our periods in a tough environment: often we are playing in 30+-degree heat, in incredible humidity, while we are being watched by tens of millions of people. We are going through equally gruelling training to compete in those circumstances, and women players can and do suffer from all sorts of physical conditions such as endometriosis (which meets the definition of a disability as defined by the *Disability Discrimination Act*), polycystic ovarian syndrome (PCOS), both of which I suffer, and horrible period pains. I can tell you, I would have played five sets over having these issues any day of the week.

A lot of girls and women don't talk about this. Because, again, there is shame around it. But it is an issue – non-negotiable – for young girls and athletes. I'll talk about this more in the next chapter, and about how we can all try to overcome this shame that leads to stigmas that hold us back.

Women's rights are human rights. Among those rights is being treated with equity and with the same respect as men.

Fertility and tennis

Women all come to a point in their lives when they must make major decisions around their fertility. And professional tennis players must decide whether they continue playing into their thirties and risk not being able to have kids.

This kind of decision is one that every woman in sport, and of course in so many workplaces, has to wrestle with. Men don't have this issue. Serena Williams is the highest-profile woman player in recent times to manage to return to tennis after having a baby – her daughter, Olympia. As a top-tier player, and one of the most respected athletes in the world, she said in an essay in *Vogue* in 2022, 'Believe me, I never wanted to have to choose between tennis and a family. I don't think it's fair. If I were a guy, I wouldn't be writing this because I'd be out there playing and winning while my wife was doing the physical labor of expanding our family.'

It's hard to step away from professional sport to have a baby if you want to come back and continue to compete afterwards. There is the challenge of not only getting back in form, but also of travelling for up to forty weeks of the year while you're on tour with your child. There is no maternity leave in tennis and other sports. And women tennis players don't just deserve maternity leave if they decide to have kids, they need it, because there is the physical challenge of coming back to elite sport after having children, and also the financial challenge of not being able to earn any money while you're on leave looking after your child and then returning having potentially lost your form and your ranking.

Female athletes have to travel with their kids on tour while trying to compete, and they have to bear the extra costs of travelling with a child. Men don't have to put their sporting career on any kind of pause. Taking all that into consideration, there should be a lot more understanding and acknowledgement of the sacrifices that women in sport have to make and how hard they have to work to participate competitively on the tour.

One measure the WTA has put into place is to give a special ranking rule to make it easier for women players to return after pregnancy: it gives a three-year protected window for new mothers so they can enter up to eight tournaments, when they get back to the circuit, using the ranking they had before they left, and they can do that for up to three years.

In 2021 the Australian Institute of Sport began a study to work out the support needed by elite sportswomen who become mothers and want to return to their career. Australian athletes said they needed good networks and strategies to make it possible to travel with a young baby, and they also wanted clear policies around pregnancy and returning to their chosen sport after having a child.

However, it seems as though most tennis players who have children while they're still playing cope by seeking advice not from our tennis and sporting bodies but from fellow players who've somehow managed to tour with children, or have supportive partners who will child-mind and problem-solve while they play. German player Tatjana Maria told a journalist at the Australian Open in 2022 that she gets asked for advice all the time: she gave birth to her daughter in 2013 and to her second in 2021 and, along with her husband, has toured with her little girls since. Her commitment and passion for both tennis and her family have shown us the incredibly tough decisions that she's had to make for both, and she has done it so well. She's a real fighter and an inspiration to female tennis players, and to women everywhere.

There are other female tennis players and women in other sports who have taken a similar route and it's a tough one. They are heroes.

So much more can and must be done to enable women to both take time off to have kids but also be able to come back to the tour and the sport they love so they can continue competing with less stress. Equal prize money at all events is one of those things that can be done and I hope we see other support come in from our sporting bodies. I would also like to see women tennis players and athletes be given access to childcare, both at tournament venues and in the hotels accommodating us during competitions.

Fertility questions

Do you have a partner? Do you have kids? Do you want kids? Are you married?

I often get asked these questions. And when I say no to all of the above, I am sometimes given a blank stare in return. I can see people want to ask, 'Why not?'

I don't mind this kind of curiosity – I am happy to discuss all sorts of issues – but the judgement that hangs in the question of *why not?* or on people's faces when I answer them honestly are not something I think I should have to accept or deal with.

For me personally, having struggled with depression, anxiety, PTSD for a very long time, I was always scared of having kids for two reasons. Firstly, because of my mental health. I wanted to heal myself and get better and I didn't want to have a child without being 100 per cent. Secondly, with my past and my childhood I was also in a way questioning, *should* I have kids? I have wondered, would having kids bring up the trauma of my own childhood?

By the time I was feeling much better in my life, which was around the age of thirty-eight, Tin and I were starting to talk about having a family and trying for a baby. We were talking about IVF, and potentially freezing my eggs. Then we broke up.

So life happens. I am now forty, and also taking into account my history of PCOS and a diagnosis of endometriosis, the reality is I am unlikely to have children now. While I am okay with that, and I might look at adoption in a few years, I do still feel like there is a massive amount of societal pressure not to be a childless woman. That something is wrong with you a) if you don't have kids and b) if you don't want to have kids.

A lot of women out there have chosen not to have kids. Perhaps they love what they do for work, perhaps they love their freedom – to be able to travel or go out for dinner or to the movies, for example, whenever they like. Perhaps they just don't have an urge to be a parent. Perhaps, like me, they had a terrible childhood which made them worried about becoming a mother themselves. Or, like me, the opportunity has gone now. Also, people might not be able to afford to have children, and let's not forget that a lot of women are wrestling with infertility issues that stop them from becoming pregnant though they want children very badly.

In November 2022 Jennifer Aniston spoke up about this when she talked to *Allure* magazine about being hounded by the media as to whether she had a baby bump, why she didn't want children, why she was so selfish, was her reluctance to have children why her marriages to Brad Pitt and Justin Theroux had broken up? In fact, she said, 'My late thirties, forties, I'd gone through really hard shit . . . I was trying to get pregnant.' It turns out that she was trying very hard to conceive but rounds and painful rounds of IVF just weren't working. Devastating for her, and made even worse because of these intrusive, incorrect assumptions being made about her childlessness.

The less we judge the better. No one should be judged for their choices. Or perhaps they weren't even choices. You never know someone's reasons or their backstory. Not having children doesn't make me, or anyone, any less of a person deserving of respect and kindness.

The lack of equity and the inequalities that women – including sportswomen – face are still massive issues in our society. So all of us – women and men – need to keep fighting to recognise and enable women's contributions to work, sport, all walks of life.

———————

Mantra: The more men and women support each other, and the less we judge each other, the better our lives will be. Women's rights are human rights and everyone should be equal.

———————

11.

SHATTERING STIGMAS

'Vulnerability sounds like truth and feels like courage. Truth and courage aren't always comfortable, but they're never weakness.'
Brené Brown

As I've grown older, I've become less afraid to talk about issues, topics and problems that many people might find uncomfortable. And, to be honest, some of the subjects I now speak about candidly I think I would never have touched as a professional athlete – for many reasons. I played in a different era, when silence really was golden, even if it was also destructive. I would argue it is not too different today. For a start, I believe there is still an expectation to be perfect placed upon our shoulders.

Vulnerability

What has motivated me to make myself vulnerable today, by speaking the truth, is essentially to shatter the myth that we have to be perfect to be 'successful'.

By 'we' I mean women in the public eye, women athletes, and in fact all of us – including women living their lives out of the scrutiny of the press but still feeling that pressure. Of course, men and boys also feel some of these pressures. But obviously I'm not well positioned to speak about men and boys, so here I want to focus on women, women in sport, and in tennis in particular.

When I first played the women's tour in the late 1990s and early 2000s, it was a time when, commercially, women's tennis was booming. We were at a stage when the fight of Billie Jean King and the Original Nine in the early 1970s was, literally, paying off.

Superstars like Venus and Serena Williams, Martina Hingis and Lindsay Davenport were all in the spotlight for their impressive athletic feats, and the marketing dollars also came their way. Not only were some of the best women players finally earning more prize money, they were being paid millions in endorsements.

But through all this – both externally and I would say internally for myself – there was a demand to be an amazing athlete *and* to be personally flawless.

194

Fast-forward ten years – same thing. We weren't to step a foot wrong. We were expected to smile on cue. If you were a young woman like me, who was experiencing a violent home life but not telling a soul, and your expression was sombre, sad, withdrawn, the media didn't like it.

It didn't just happen to me, it happened to too many of us.

During this time, it seemed to me that you were not to talk privately or publicly about weakness, you were not to show vulnerability.

When I played, and I believe this is still the case today, weakness was the worst thing you could show, both off and on the court. It felt as though it would be disastrous if you showed a hint of emotional vulnerability to the press or really just in general after a match. There was no serious talk of mental health issues on the tennis circuit. That is, of showing you were human. Also, because of sponsors having such a big influence on the players they were supporting, anything less than perfect was not acceptable. I believe this was the case outside of sport as well.

I think this is incredibly dangerous, putting unattainable expectations on us. To me, it is in fact extremely helpful to show we are not perfect, that we are vulnerable, so people can identify with us. A few months after Roger Federer retired in September 2022, he said he now realised how much pressure he'd had on his shoulders through his tennis career, and that he believed the intensity of the tour was having a negative impact on many players' mental health: 'The tour is tough . . . travel, practice, jetlag. Nobody is allowed to say, "Oh, I'm tired today," because it looks like you're weak, and that's why players sometimes end up having mental-health problems. You're supposed to show strength. But we're also not machines, we're also just human beings.'

I agree so much with Roger: we are not super-human as tennis players. And we should be encouraged by our peers, our teams, the tennis authorities and by sponsors to speak up. Surely sending players to breaking point is a terrible example for anyone who loves the sport, or anyone at all.

Certainly, though, I grew up in an environment that demanded you not show your true feelings.

Why?

I still think there are many athletes, not just in tennis but outside of tennis, who are going through a lot in their lives, but they don't talk about it because it makes them feel ashamed, or they are scared they will be publicly shamed or lose sponsors, or appear weak to competitors.

If you are an athlete, and you show 'weakness', well, you will have given up the tough exterior that most feel they need to succeed. You will have given away that edge to your opponents, which no one wants to do.

Whether you are a public figure or not, what should be celebrated is talking about your issues, because it takes so much guts and bravery and courage to open up on whatever may have affected you, be it depression, child abuse, sexual abuse, eating disorders. That should be praised, especially when it comes to athletes, who so many young people look up to as role models.

In the last few years some players have started to open up about their struggles with mental health and they've been supported by their fans, so I hope others can see that this kind of discussion can be really positive and set a great example for younger players. For kids, for everyone. A lot of former and current players thanked me, after they'd read my first book, for talking so openly about my struggles.

In 2022 Canadian player Bianca Andreescu, the 2019 US Open champion, decided to take six months off. She was injured after her 2019 win at Flushing Meadows, and didn't play in 2020. Then COVID hit. She was ready to play again at the beginning of 2021, but a series of unfortunate events (her coach got COVID and she was sent into hard lockdown in a hotel room in Abu Dhabi, which meant no practice for two weeks) led to her losing in the first round of the Australian Open. Things spiralled from there, until at the end of that year she decided to take some time out. She said later: 'I literally wanted to quit this sport. It was so bad. I didn't want to hear about tennis, or think about tennis, or anything even close to it for the first three months I was away.' However, after a few months, her mindset to play returned and she found her peace again, and her form.

A similar case: in May 2023, American Amanda Anisimova, who reached the French Open semi-finals in 2019 aged only nineteen, announced she was taking a break from tennis. 'I've really been struggling with my mental health and burnout since the summer of 2022,' she posted on Instagram. 'It's become unbearable being at tennis tournaments. At this point my priority is my mental well-being and taking a break for some time. I've worked as hard as I could to push through it.'

At a certain stage in an athlete's career, especially when so many of us start playing professional tennis from an incredibly young age, I think for sure it's a good idea to take a break, either to recover from physical or mental health problems, or to get some perspective away from the pressure of competing.

Ash Barty took an eighteen-month break because she felt she'd started playing so young, and she wanted to experience some normal teenage life: 'It was too much too quickly for me as I've been travelling from quite a young age,' she said. She returned to the tour, but then retired in March 2022, when her career was on a high. Even Ash, an incredible champion, had decided she'd had enough of the tennis circuit, saying she no longer had 'the physical drive, the emotional want and everything it takes to challenge yourself at the very top of the level any more. I am spent.'

I'd interviewed Ash a couple of months before this, when she'd just got into the second round of the Australian Open. I'm a huge fan of hers so I found myself getting emotional as we talked and I told her how proud she'd made all Australians after her win at Wimbledon the year before. I'd made a point of praising her parents after that 2021 win, saying I hoped they would set an example for parents in Australia and around the world: 'This is how you support [players]. You don't pressure them, you're there for them and this is why she is there.'

What Ash did, to follow her heart and happiness by retiring early, but also taking a break earlier, were really brave and mature decisions – putting her mental health first, rather than the win-at-all-costs attitude that can be so destructive in the end. What she has done I think will be an example on how to navigate a career.

In 2021, Naomi Osaka wrote an article in TIME magazine where she observed, 'It has become apparent to me that literally everyone either suffers from issues related to their mental health or knows someone who does . . . I do hope that people can relate and understand it's O.K. to not be O.K., and it's O.K. to talk about it. There are people who can help, and there is usually light at the end of any tunnel.'

So, slowly things are hopefully changing in this space but we all need to work on making sure that athletes can feel more comfortable to open up. Everybody needs to be more empathetic and encouraging for athletes to feel safe to talk about things like mental health. I feel passionately that I want to always keep playing my part in doing this as a retired player who has the perspective of having been on the tennis circuit but also now can look at it critically from the outside. Your own mental health and wellbeing is the most important thing – that's what I want athletes to know and always be aware of. Managers, sponsors and coaches should also bear this in mind and have the understanding that athletes need to be safe and have their physical and mental health cared for. Even outside tennis and professional sport, the same thing goes for any sporting club, school or workplace – there should be support structures in place to safeguard people's mental health.

Periods

I've realised recently that there is something I would never have talked about in my playing days because of the stigma and shame attached to it, and that is menstruation.

Why are we not talking much more about what women go through every single month? The subject did come up at Wimbledon in 2022 because of the rule that women competitors must wear white. That rule has been around for 150 years, and finally enough players complained about it that the tournament was forced, later in the year, to revise it. The tournament said that from 2023 women and girls could wear dark-coloured undershorts under their white skirt, 'provided they are no longer than their shorts or skirt'. And that 'It is our hope that this rule adjustment will help players focus purely on their performance by relieving a potential source of anxiety.'

One of the first times I played at Wimbledon, aged sixteen, I was dealing with having my period, while competing on one of the most prestigious tennis stages. The place where they demanded you wear white. It didn't occur to me to question that rule back then – I don't think any woman on the tour questioned it – but I remember being almost paralysed by fear of what would happen if I had a leak. If red spots would mark my white dress, my underwear. If I sat down and left a mark on the towel. How would I handle the embarrassment? Would I lose my focus? Would it cost me the match? Sometimes I would take a toilet break purely to check that everything was okay, that I hadn't leaked.

I had no one to talk to about it, and it was definitely not a matter anyone spoke about publicly. But it was something we were worried about. You would use tampons, pads, and three pairs of underwear.

In the last couple of years, female athletes in other sports have also begun to talk about this worry. The paranoia of leaking, piled on top of competing on live TV in front of tens of millions of people, is not fun. The pressure is immense. Even if you are turning up to a local court for a casual hit of tennis, or to a pool to swim laps, the stress associated with menstruation and sport is full-on. And the more we talk about this, the less embarrassment there is, and the more others – especially men – can understand what we are going through.

In 2022 in the UK a group of fifty female elite athletes banded together to urge people to #SayPeriod rather than using other words for the natural way our bodies work. The campaign was all about ditching language like 'Aunt Flow', 'girls' stuff', words that encourage the stigma around periods. Older women even used to call their periods 'the curse'. This kind of language helps no one.

English swimmer Hannah Miley, a former Olympic champion, spoke candidly about how, when she was training and competing, periods were viewed as a problem rather than what your body naturally goes through: 'It was very hush, hush and as a swimmer, you are very exposed as well, so if you start without it being planned, or if you have a leak-through, it is very obvious,' Miley told *Sky Sports News*. 'It can feel horrendous as the water just makes the blood look so much more than it actually is.

'But I had a real issue, [my period] was really heavy, really painful, and it was impacting how I was competing. I was feeling like I was very lethargic, I'd become anaemic as well. I was just training really, really hard and it was just impacting everything I was doing.'

At the 2022 European Championships sprinter Dina Asher-Smith spoke about being unable to complete a race due to period pain. 'More people need to actually research it from a sports science perspective because it's absolutely huge,' she told the BBC.

'I feel like if it was a men's issue, we'd have a million different ways to combat things, but with women, there just needs to be more funding in that area.'

There's no doubt your period affects your performance (on top of that, where we play is often hot and humid) and I agree with Dina – if this was something men went through, there'd probably have been decades of sports science expertise poured into it by now. I never felt as physically strong during certain days of my cycle. And as someone who has endometriosis and PCOS, for a long time I suffered from heavy periods, pain and cramping for those days. Sometimes I would be in the foetal position on the floor from the severity of my abdominal pain. I didn't know it wasn't normal to have that kind of thing going on. I had it all my playing career.

There needs to be more understanding around our bodies, not least by tournament organisers. The simple issues of having tampons and sanitary pads easily available at tournaments would be a great start. While we do have these at the professional level, they are not always available at junior tournaments, which is a big miss. And for everyone up until 2019, here in Australia we were still paying GST on pads and tampons. I think that was outrageous.

Breaking mental health stigmas

The first step I took, before I wrote *Unbreakable*, towards talking about my mental health battles was in an interview in 2009.

A couple of months before that interview, I'd had the Australian Open of my dreams and afterwards the media attention was huge. My management decided to tee me up with one exclusive interview with the *Sydney Morning Herald*'s dedicated sports magazine *Sport & Style*. So in April 2009 in Miami I met up with Australian journalist Jessica Halloran for a profile. Obviously I had no idea then that Jess and I would end up talking for much longer than just the duration of that interview as she has now co-written two books with me. Back then I was twenty-six, I was feeling the highs of my comeback, I was in a good place but still feeling vulnerable at times despite the on-court glory.

Sport & Style arranged an amazing fashion photoshoot (one of the photographs taken by renowned fashion photographer Simon Upton was later used as the cover shot for *Unbreakable*).

The interview took place in a bar at the hotel where I was staying and as I sat drinking Diet Coke, I shared more than I had in any other interview. I explained that part of the reason I'd left my family unit was to escape the mental and physical abuse I'd experienced. I did not go into detail, but I gave more away than ever before that something very damaging had happened to me. 'I've been through a lot worse than anybody on the tour. I can say that with confidence,' I said. 'There was a period where there was nothing that could make me happy. I wanted somebody else's life.'

The point I'd like to make is that I think that although I've always been a naturally vulnerable person, an open person, it took time to get really comfortable making my story public. As you know, nowadays I remain so passionate about breaking the stigma around mental health, and our struggles with it. I know the power of breaking this stigma. It is a primary reason for my motivational speaking.

I now know that carrying around pain inside is dangerous and very detrimental to us. The Black Dog Institute itself says that 'mental health stigmas are still real and have a devastating effect'. It advocates strongly for people to speak up to minimise the stigma around mental health; that doing so is essential to creating a safe and inclusive world for Australians living with a mental illness.

Stigmas and myths

The Black Dog Institute explains that stigmas start from myths and misunderstandings. And that they can manifest in many forms – be it exclusion, silence, labelling. The institute strongly advises us to stop using words that are associated with poor mental health in thoughtless ways. For example, saying things to people like 'You can't be depressed, you're so bubbly.' 'She's schizophrenic.' 'Just snap out of it!' 'You'll be fine – think positively.'

According to their website, one in five Australians will experience a mental illness in 2023 and more than half of those with a mental illness will not seek help.

Why? Society has historically viewed mental illness as a sign of weakness – not a real disease.

And these stigmas still exist today. People who have a mental illness feel ashamed. They hide. They don't get the help or treatment they need.

As the Black Dog Institute says, it's *essential* that we speak up about these stigmas. They are costing lives.

In 2023, I started writing open letters to the community of people who follow me on Instagram, including a post on recognising the signs of diminishing mental health, and how it is important to try to think carefully about these. I said:

Dokic_Jelena ✔

These are some of the things that help me recognise and realise if my mental health is not where it needs to be and if I am struggling again:

– I am struggling to get out of bed

– I am isolating myself

– My home is messy

– I am overwhelmed, irritable, anxious and I have no patience

– Feeling guilty or worthless

– I am not responding to family and friends

– Loss of interest in activities and hobbies

– Feeling sad

– Fatigue, where daily tasks feel difficult or take longer to do like getting dressed or running simple errands.

These are some of the things I experience if my mental health is getting bad.

It is so important to know what those signs are for you so that you can do something about it as soon as possible.

One of the things that I do if I feel this is happening is go for walks and connect with nature. Spend some time outside in the fresh air.

Whatever works for you do it and look out for those signs so that you can react on time.

I hope this was helpful for someone out there.

The next day I did a follow-up on what helps:

Dokic_Jelena ✓

So following on from my post yesterday, as promised I will talk more about it today.

It's important to know what the signs are if you are feeling mentally and emotionally exhausted and it's also important to know what you can do immediately to be able to help yourself.

What are some of the signs that you might be exhausted?

Shattering stigmas

These are some of mine:

– I feel irritable and I am moody

– I can't stop thinking about work or what I still have to do

– I feel drained

– My hobbies and fun things start to feel like chores and I have no motivation to do them

– My bag, house, suitcase, makeup bag is unorganised and I don't have the energy to organise it

– I feel like or I do cry for no particular reason

– I am dragging in the morning and it takes me a lot longer to get going

– Isolating myself from other people. Friends, coworkers, loved ones

– Procrastinating and postponing things that I have to do like emailing and texting back, finishing off small tasks and errands

– No energy or motivation to exercise

Some simple self care ideas if I am feeling exhausted. For me those are:

– Go to bed earlier than usual

– Nap whenever I can

– Ask for help

Fearless

– Turn off my phone and social media even if it's just for half hour

– Spend time in the sun, nature

– Light and short walk. Even just 10 minutes outside

– Sit or lay on the grass and watch the sky and/or close my eyes and just be.

– Light some candles in my living room

– Go swimming for fun not exercise

– Have a cup of coffee, tea, hot chocolate or a fresh squeezed juice

– Sit and be still for 10 minutes

– Watch the sunrise or sunset, don't take any pictures, use your phone or put it on social media. Just watch it and enjoy it

– Do a picnic by myself or with a friend in the park or on the beach

– Go to a cafe, order a coffee and/or breakfast and just sit and be. Enjoy it, no phone, no distractions just sit and enjoy

– Binge watch my favourite show

– Take a bath

– Write down 3 things I am grateful for

I hope this helps. Also, don't forget that you are doing amazing and doing the best you can.

Make sure you give yourself credit.

Take care of yourselves.

Domestic violence stigma

Many people who are suffering or have survived domestic violence feel an enormous amount of shame.

I have reflected often on why victims feel this devastating shame. I certainly had to get past a whole heap to be able to tell my story in *Unbreakable*. While I was writing it I still had great fear and embarrassment around what I'd suffered at my father's hands. I remained gripped by the terror that my father had instilled in me about speaking up.

There are many complex reasons for abuse survivors to feel shame. For me, my Eastern European background was relevant to why I kept quiet. Within that culture, the idea of talking about something that makes you feel vulnerable or something that is not considered perfect is shameful. It's considered a weakness, an embarrassment to your family and community, and it's the same in many other cultures.

My father knew how to make me feel ashamed. As you know, he would constantly belittle and mock me, tell me how useless I was, on and off the court, even after big wins. Being a runner-up was completely unacceptable. I learnt this early at the courts where I trained in White City. As I wrote in *Unbreakable*:

One day I lose the final of a tournament in White City. This is seen as a failing in my father's eyes. He's in a mood, he's already hurled a truckload of verbal abuse at me on the walk to the station, and we are now standing on the platform at Edgecliff. He suddenly snatches my losing crystal trophy out of my hand and pelts it into a nearby brick wall. The sound of glass breaking echoes around the station as it smashes, causing a bunch of commuters to turn to see what's happened. I crouch to try to pick up the fragments on the platform. I put them in a nearby trash can while everyone is sadly watching on. I felt utterly ashamed and miserable.

But some of the hardest episodes of shame to try to erase from my memory are when my father used to make me take off my top and struck me over and over with a belt. When I recounted this for my book I felt nothing but pain in telling it. It still hurts now, though I've related it many times. That kind of behaviour is so humiliating and demeaning.

The shame is only worsened by having to endure questions about, in my case, why I didn't tell anyone sooner about what my father was doing to me, and in other cases – when women don't leave their abusive partners – why these women stay in violent households.

These questions show the stigma and, honestly, lack of understanding and knowledge that family violence survivors must endure. It is important to understand that there is great fear in those suffering intimate partner violence – shame and fear around speaking up, and often terror around leaving such households. The worst thing we can do is blame survivors for staying silent, to judge them for not leaving. It's victim-blaming. It's the perpetrators who need to be condemned.

When it comes to family violence the script needs to change; instead of shame, we need to flip it – give credit to, and believe, those who can speak up. We need to recognise the courage it takes for people to tell their story.

We must help and believe women and children who report suffering violence, in any way we can, whether it's listening to them, or lobbying governments to fund vitally important resources for them such as shelters, access to money on leaving violent situations, or housing, basic hygienic needs like pads and tampons for women and their daughters, nappies, and mobile phones.

These issues came up in *Q&A* in February 2023 and one question was about accessing superannuation. I made the point that one of the reasons among many that women don't leave abusive households and partners is that they are terrified they won't be able to start again, financially, or with housing; or any of these basic needs. I acknowledged that when I was nineteen and left my family, I was lucky because I was a professional athlete on tour, I had the ability to keep earning a living in the same way I had been doing, but even so there was a huge amount of pressure because my father had all my savings, so I was starting again from the ground up. A statistic that shocked me is that 90 per cent of women who leave their abusive situations are forced to return within four weeks because they are unable to start over.

In a situation where women don't have anything to fall back on as I did, perhaps it is a good idea for them to be able to access their superannuation and withdraw some money to help them to their feet and to have some financial backing when they desperately need it. Otherwise these women may not even make it to retirement. And if people have this option – to take control of their situation, rather than relying always on state support, which is often lacking anyway – at least it's empowering for them and might take away some of the shame and helplessness that you feel after being beaten down for years.

I want to encourage more unashamed conversations around topics like family violence, struggles with mental health, and other subjects in and out of sport that not a lot of people like to speak of. The more we talk about what is happening in our society when it comes to violence, the more we have the power to help destigmatise what's occurring behind closed doors, and to help the vulnerable.

I have said it many times in this book: speaking up creates change, saves lives.

And the more people can listen empathetically to survivor stories like mine and many others', the better. That's what I am fighting for: normalising hard conversations around difficult issues.

The last thing I want to say on this is that if you know someone going through an abusive situation, show up for them. Be there for them; call them, give them a hug, listen.

Mantra: I want to end with another Brené Brown quote . . . 'We don't have to do all of it alone. We were never meant to.'

12.

HAPPINESS, HEALING AND KINDNESS

'Very little is needed to make a happy life, it is all within yourself, in your way of thinking.'
Marcus Aurelius Antoninus

Therapy has given me an opportunity to take a breath, understand myself better and to establish a new set of values to live by, ones that feel meaningful, and I hope will enrich my life and give me a level of contentment.

Today, this is what I value

- Joy, happiness and the feeling of success of doing something I love.
- Having the right people around me.

- Having a safe space to talk and make sense of life.
- The small pleasures: a coffee and walk with a friend. Watching the sunrise. Taking a swim in the ocean.
- Being grateful. Living in the moment.
- Today, I value simple things in life.

The value of money

As you know, when I was a young child my family struggled financially, not only when we lived in Europe, but also after we moved to Australia. My clothes often came from second-hand shops. My shoes had holes in them. I never had fancy tennis clothes like some of the other girls did at White City, the tennis centre where I played in Sydney's beautiful Eastern Suburbs.

Although we had little money, some of my earliest memories are of my father talking about it all the time. That is, how I could and would make money for our family. That tennis would provide us with an avenue out of poverty. I grew up with the idea that if I could make enough money, my father and in turn my entire family would finally be happy.

Now, I wasn't sure exactly what that feeling of 'absolute happiness' was, but I knew it wasn't this tenuous existence I was living out as a kid.

In my environment, being successful in matches was all that mattered. Fortunately, as you know, I loved tennis. Adored everything about it. I never desired the money I could possibly make from the sport, but as a young girl I did hope that if I made enough money, it might mean an end to our problems and the abuse.

As I got older, however, because of my father's attitude to my winnings, and seeing that they didn't change his behaviour, I knew in my heart that material wealth might not transform our family, or make my father love me.

One of the first times I earned prize money from playing tennis came in October 1998. I had entered one of my first international tournaments, an International Tennis Federation (ITF), challenger-level, in Saga, on the Japanese island of Kyushu. I was a young teenager, fifteen, and travelling with my coach at the time, Lesley Bowrey.

On the 1998 tour of Asia, the results of Lesley's coaching and mentoring were paying off. I was feeling confident as a player and had worked my heart out to make it through four rounds of qualifying to get into the main draw. There, my successful run continued. I got to the final, beating the No. 1 seed in the tournament, who was ranked around 100 in the WTA rankings. I made a small amount of prize money for this.

The next tournament I went to was the Thailand Open, where I was ranked 362. I smashed through three tough qualifying rounds, playing the world No. 23 at the time, Julie Halard-Decugis, in the first round. I lost this match, and although I don't like losing I felt okay and happy with my performance.

Then everything went to shit. At Bangkok Airport after the match my father called. His care wasn't on my effort this time but on something that would become a running theme – the dollars.

'How much money have you made?' he barked down the line.

'I don't know,' I said.

He demanded that I count my winnings. So in the middle of the busy airport lounge I placed all the American dollars on the floor and started counting. (Back in 1998 we were paid in cash for the smaller prize money.)

Lesley asked me what I was doing. I told her that my father needed to know how much money I'd made. I felt panicked. I had the threat of him from thousands of miles away. She tried to stop me but I refused until I'd got to the total. It was 700 US dollars.

I gave my father the money when I arrived home to Fairfield. He greeted the cash gruffly, no thanks.

This moment set the tone for the rest of my playing career. I never kept a cent of my winnings – my father had control over them. He'd once said that the aim was for me to make a million dollars. So after the trip to Thailand, I had it in my mind that if I could just do that, he would calm down and in turn be more settled at home. He would stop abusing me and just let me play tennis.

That did not happen.

As the years passed, such was my lack of interest in material things and money that when I was severing my ties with my father, I signed over to him our tennis ranch in Florida, as well as millions I had made in my career up to that point. My future earnings? I signed them over too.

Why? I hoped he would leave me alone if he had the money he seemed so greedy for.

If my father weaponised money, at least in doing so he showed me that financial wealth doesn't always change things for the better. There are fundamentals that are more important, ones that strengthen both our own lives and the lives of others, and can actually bring us joy.

The joy of doing something we love

After some therapy, I started to openly ask myself the question, what actually brings me happiness? I can say I hadn't really even thought about this until the age of thirty-nine, but something happened in a therapy session in August 2022 that was an *ah-ha* moment for me.

I was exploring deeply how I have viewed life and my psychiatrist explained that my lens tends to be a dark one. He encouraged me to think about happiness, and about what was good in my life.

I can't change what happened to me. With this in mind, he encouraged me to start to formally reframe my difficult past as something that can be used to educate others. It was almost as though he were endorsing the work I was doing at that time – writing my book, and the motivational speaking I'd taken on after its publication. So in this session he brought clarity and legitimacy to how I was living – and this was powerful for me. I was so lost after I gave up tennis that it was deeply encouraging to hear him tell me that the ways in which I had decided to replace tennis were not only potentially helping my mental health journey but also worthwhile for others.

In my life as a professional athlete up until 2013, securing victory was everything. Winning, therefore, made me happy. It gave me a purpose. Now I look back on my tennis career,

I see that I regarded a win, or at least being really good at the sport, as equating to some form of happiness. And after leaving the tennis circuit, happiness and values didn't figure in my thoughts – I was just surviving day to day as I tried to find a new purpose.

When I look back and reflect on the world I once existed in, I can see that I lived in a constant state of *wanting*; that is, wanting to win the next point, game, set, match; wanting to win the next match in tournaments or grand slams. The tennis world is a lonely, extremely competitive scene, and not only on the court. Such a brutal, materialistic world can very easily make you lose your sense of what's actually important in life.

Over the past six years, during which I have established my television career, I think my perspective on what's important, and on joy, happiness and success, has changed completely from when I was an athlete.

My life is no longer about chasing the next win.
I do my job because I have a deep passion for it.

I loved being a highly successful tennis player – even with my father's destructive ways happening in the background, I did manage to compartmentalise enough to still love my work on the court. Tennis was my passion, my love, it always will be, regardless of my father. But tennis is also a world that can easily distract you from the important values in life because of how ruthless it is and because of all the money players are competing for.

So let's move on to the next one that's near the top of my list, and very possibly yours too.

Having the right people around

When I was a young teenager trying to make a name for myself on the circuit, my father did a rare good thing for me and employed Lesley Bowrey as my coach. She was a no-nonsense, fair, tough coach with the warmest of hearts. I met her at White City tennis courts soon after arriving in Australia from Serbia, and she was the first person not only to take notice of me but actually to care for me.

She had seen me furiously hitting a ball against a grey wall at White City in the afternoons before my squad training. I know she admired my work ethic from afar and soon I was on junior tennis teams of which she was the travelling coach. Next, we toured overseas for world junior competitions, and then she became my personal coach.

She was great for my tennis, and also a mother-type figure to me. I came to be certain that she cared deeply for me as a person, not just as a tennis player.

Lesley had once been one of the best players in the world. Over a two-decade career from the late 1950s until the late 1970s, she won the singles title at the French Open in 1963 and '65, and she got to No. 2 in the world rankings of women's singles players in 1964.

Lesley drilled me, she was tough on me, but she was also kind and we always had fun. I think that this period with her – and when we were away from my home base in Fairfield travelling for tennis – were the happiest times of my tennis life.

Why?

She worked me hard – we both shared this hunger to train our hearts out – but she also allowed me to share my real self. That person I usually buried deep inside, the mischievous, mildly cheeky, fun and light-hearted teen. Lesley reinforced the truth to me that adults don't have to be cruel to get the best out of you. It was under her tutelage that I started to really shine on the tennis courts. We would also sightsee during tournaments, which made me really happy – I'd never done anything like that with my parents.

She believed in me. Her belief made me believe in myself.

She was the Fed Cup captain and backed me, as a fifteen-year-old, to win the singles matches against two top-hundred Argentinian players. The press went ballistic when I did that. I won the junior US Open with her by my side. In 1998 I finished the year ranked as the junior world No. 1. I went to the Hopman Cup in January 1999 and won it, teaming up with fellow young gun Mark Philippoussis and with Lesley in my corner.

A few weeks later, before the 1999 Australian Open, Lesley invited me to stay with her and her husband, Bill (also one of the best players in the world at one stage – he was ranked world No. 8 in 1967 and he won the Australian Open singles title in 1968). With them, I prepared for the Australian Open. Every morning we went running along the Yarra River. Every day we sat down around their dining room table in South Yarra and had interesting, calm conversations about tennis and life. I saw my first glimpse of normality. That not everyone's house was filled with fear and terror. I saw the other side of family life. I wanted it.

Then, after five days of bliss, my dream world was shattered: my father arrived in Melbourne and I was ordered by him to stay with him.

It was the most awful day when my father insisted that I (not him) sack Lesley after that 1999 Australian Open. I will never forget having to tell her she would no longer be coaching me. It was shattering and I felt sick about it for years. I still do.

Now, although the memory still sickens me, I am eternally grateful for the time and effort that Lesley put in to training and mentoring me over the years, not only on the tennis court, but in my life.

And of course there's Todd. Todd is one of the greatest doubles players ever, and he was a significant force on the singles circuit – he was ranked No. 19 in the world in 1997. He and his fellow Aussie Mark Woodforde won an awe-inspiring five Wimbledon titles between 1993 and '97; overall he won sixteen grand slam men's doubles – nine Wimbledons, three US Opens, three Australian Opens and one French Open – and six mixed doubles grand slams. He was ranked No. 1 for 204 weeks of his career. He also won a gold medal at the 1996 Olympics in Atlanta and a silver in Sydney in 2000.

Ten years ago Todd sat me down in a café at the National Tennis Centre in Melbourne and asked me what my plans were beyond tennis.

'I'm not sure,' I replied. 'Maybe commentary?' But I had a lot of fear about how I could ever make that happen.

Todd has mentored me tirelessly. He encouraged me to write *Unbreakable*. He has instilled belief in me and advocated for me. I am so thankful to have someone like him on my side, not only professionally but also as a friend.

My long-time manager, David Malina, with whom I've had an association for more than a decade, is another person who's consistently believed in me. He was there for me, even post-tennis career, when few others were, encouraging me to write my first book and branch out into commentary. He too was there for me after my break-up with Tin.

So was my friend Herme. She took my calls all through the period after Tin and I split, and listened with her deep heart. When we met we clicked immediately. I think that's because we actually have quite a bit in common. She hasn't had an easy life, but she's a fighter, she's worked hard, and she has accomplished so much in her career. She's a successful, busy woman but always finds the time and generosity to wish me the best when I'm setting up to do a big interview, or am apprehensive about something in my life. She's full of humanity and kindness, and I see her now almost a bit like an older sister who encourages me and supports me when I need it. She always puts others first despite the adversity she's been through; I find it inspiring how she's dealt with the difficult parts of her past and maintained a great passion for life.

Having the right people on my side means for me having a safe space to talk and make sense of life. My past has meant that doing that up to now has been pretty hard. So, finding the psychiatrist I have, sharing my story with him and going deep inwards to try to mend the trauma, have been critical steps towards healing and finding peace.

Connections of this kind, as well as with my friends and mentors, is therefore one of my most cherished values.

The small pleasures

In 2022 I went on holiday to Croatia. I still have family there and I wanted to see them, as well as getting the chance for some downtime. I was there to relax after a year when I was still dealing with my separation from Tin, and to visit my mother and spend some time with my brother.

In the quiet of this holiday I thought more about what makes me happy, how I want to live, how to prioritise and define my values in the future.

If you know me, I have a mischievous temperament at times. I like to joke around and have fun. Despite all that's happened to me, personally I think of myself as someone who cherishes joy. Lesley brought out this side of me, but when my father removed her from my life, it took years for it to re-emerge again, having been stifled by the violent household I lived in.

On this trip I really started to concentrate on trying to find happiness in the stillness of the holiday and appreciating its small moments. I was so relaxed that I drank an Aperol Spritz at sundown. (If you know me, you will know this is a rare occurrence. I almost never drink.)

I would wake up just before dawn to get a coffee by myself in Dubrovnik Old Town and enjoy the sunrise.

The saying 'collect moments not things' resonated with me on that trip. I wrote this Instagram post one morning to try to express how I was feeling:

Dokic_Jelena ✅

No makeup, sunscreen on my face, salt in my hair and a bucket hat by the sea.

Absolute bliss.

Oh how the small things in life and the ones we sometimes take for granted actually bring us so much joy.

So here is some food for thought:

Make your life about joy and happiness.

Enjoy that morning coffee.

Watch the sunrise. Watch the sunset.

Spend time in nature.

Say hello with a smile. Be kind.

Find something to smile about every day:
a beautiful sunny day, having five minutes to yourself, a coffee with a friend, a walk by the beach or in the park . . .

Enjoy the little things: good coffee, a tasty nourishing meal, cup of tea on the balcony, reading a book, watching your favourite TV show, walking the dog, a dip in the sea or pool . . .

Celebrate your small and big wins and accomplishments.

Learn and grow every single day.

Be kind to others.

Appreciate others being kind to you.

Inspire and be inspired.

Because life is too short to spend it not enjoying even the smallest things and the smallest wins.

So try and live a life of gratitude, kindness, enjoyment and trying to find joy and happiness whenever and wherever you can even in the smallest things.

Sending you all lots of love and hugs and I hope you find something that makes you smile today and I hope you find something that gives you joy today.

Toxic positivity

We all know that life is not just sunshine and rainbows. Recovering from a traumatic life event, or a traumatic childhood, is a difficult, confronting, painful process. For many of us, I'm sure that healing has us ugly-crying far too often.

Dealing with trauma is messy. Healing is messy. There's nothing easy about it. Nothing pretty about it either.

Perhaps you know people who have turned to you when you are struggling and said something along the lines of, 'We should always look on the bright side' or 'Just stay positive.'

There is something problematic about this kind of advice; *especially* the one I think is the worst of all: 'You have to get over it.'

When I heard about 'toxic positivity', the idea of it really clicked for me and I wanted to know more. I'm a big advocate of trying to practise gratitude, and I know the value from my counselling sessions of keeping a log of good things that have happened or are happening to me, but at the same time, when the darkness gets on top of me, having someone acknowledge that it's valid to be struggling, that I'm not just wallowing in self-pity, is of huge value.

Toxic positivity is when people make no room for those challenging emotions, and brush them away. Apparently, the idea came out of the US where, in the 1980s, research was done on the unrealistic optimism that was being put forward as helpful to people's mental health – when in fact it was, is, not.

Bestselling author, athlete and mindset coach Turia Pitt has made some excellent points about toxic positivity. As you know, Turia is someone I and many other people regard as an all-round inspiration. And I have been fortunate enough to meet her, as well as appear on her podcast 'Turia Pitt is Hard Work'.

If you're not familiar with Turia, she's incredible and has an epic story of survival. In 2011, while competing in an ultra-marathon, she was caught in a fierce grassfire and badly burnt. She lost seven fingers, had over two hundred medical procedures and spent two harrowing years in recovery. Yet since then she's competed in many gruelling physical challenges and nowadays she coaches people – physically and mentally. I admire all her achievements so much, but it's her mindset I most admire.

She has spoken up in the past about the damaging effects of toxic positivity. In an interview with the *Weekend Australian* magazine in early 2023 Turia had this to say about it:

A big part of getting on ... isn't just about pulling your socks up and stiffening your upper lip but acknowledging that you're not always going to feel amazing every day, and that's OK. I think there's this culture of toxic positivity where we all have this pressure to always feel amazing, be motivated and super enthusiastic. I think that's bullshit. Life isn't always roses and butterflies and we've got to be OK with that.

Turia's blunt approach is spot-on. Another thing she said on this subject really resonated with me:

There's this culture of toxic positivity nowadays, where if something bad happens to us we've just got to kill it with positivity and everything will turn out well ... But we're missing a crucial step of just acknowledging that something terrible happened, grieving and allowing yourself to just be for a moment.

If you speak to any psychological expert, they will say that suppressing emotions, rejecting the bad emotions, can actually be harmful in the long run. It can prevent you from processing them, and therefore from overcoming the problem in front of you. Which is exactly what I did for a long time. The cycle of life means you'll have tough moments, tough situations. You'll have to face loss. And so you have to accept this. So 'it will be all right' is not a good message to send out to people. Some will have to find ways to get out of tough situations – there's really no escaping that reality.

When I appeared on Turia's podcast in May 2022, we got on very well, partly because we both come from a similar place when it comes to our attitude to life. Probably our greatest common ground is we are both unafraid to speak our mind. We are both brutally honest. We got chatting on everything from body-shaming to surviving an abusive home.

As we spoke, I made this point to Turia, 'The pain and the scars, I think in a way, they're a part of me. They're a part of my story . . . The past doesn't have to define me, but it's a part of me. It's made me who I am and you know what, it's made me a pretty strong person.'

It's also important to remember that when something difficult comes up, how we deal with it is key – how and when we manage our emotions. Life's struggles do leave scars. But we must have hope that even with them, we can continue to lead a productive, good life.

The power of story

During the last couple of years, as I have tried to recover not only from an enormous break-up, but also from the ongoing trauma of my childhood and youth, I have had some surprising moments. One of the biggest came in February 2023. I was talking to my psychiatrist and I was telling him how good I was feeling. That my work was going well, I was booked out for talks, and I felt great when I addressed audiences with my keynote speech (which is a condensed version of my life story so far). I told him how, every time I told my story, in front of hundreds of people, I felt really good about myself. I said, 'The more I do it, the more I feel better about myself.'

And he said, 'That's because you are talking about your life. It's called narrative therapy. You are unpacking it. And when you keep doing that, when you keep talking about it, all this weight is being lifted. You're dealing with your trauma. Just like you did with *Unbreakable*.'

Everything really made sense to me at that moment. He explained that narrative therapy is a psychological approach that seeks to adjust the stories we tell about our life in order to bring about positive change and better mental health. *Psychology Today* describes it as working when we view the events that occur over time in our lives as stories, some of which stand out as more significant or more fateful than others:

These significant stories, usually stemming from negative events, can ultimately shape one's identity. Beyond this identity, the narrative therapist views a client's life as multitiered and full of possibilities that are just waiting to be discovered. The therapist does not act as the expert, but rather helps clients see how they are the experts regarding their own life and how they can uncover the dreams, values, goals, and skills that define who they are, separate from their problems. These are the buried stories that can be rewritten and woven into the ongoing and future stories of their lives.

It actually really makes sense because that's where healing started for me – with writing my first book. Rather than being a victim, I started to see myself as a survivor.

The speaking circuit gives me another chance to set free heavy issues I have been carrying around inside me – again, rather than keeping my abuser's secrets, I am telling my story to empower and inspire others.

What I know is that I feel a lot better than I have in a long time. My friends tell me I am more confident, I am a more centred person, calmer and really just better at managing the highs and lows that life can throw at you. I know myself I am handling things better than I ever did before.

Acceptance

One of the biggest things for me in the last year has been, quite simply, acceptance.

You can only control the controllables.

When I have been in a bad space, I have been able to process my trauma better, accept it rather than fight it and ruminate on whatever difficult time I am having rather than trying to move through it as quickly as I can.

I am now, with help, developing the life skills to move through the hard times. And if you look at the time it took me to unpack and publicly tell my story of being abused (fifteen years) and then finally to get professional help recently – I have come a long way.

What I know for myself now (and, look, I accept that this may not be for everyone) is that you *can* heal from bad things, or at the least learn to manage the fall-out from them, while becoming a kinder and more resilient person. In essence, the worst of times can in fact encourage growth. But – and this is a big BUT – this is not to say I am fully healed. What I know now is that the worst events have shaped my identity. However, they are not who I am.

Like I said earlier, life is not always all sunshine and rainbows. It certainly isn't for me. I am pretty strong yet still I have some bad days. There are days when I'm paralysed by depressive thoughts, wanting to shut out the entire world. I have woken up in the morning and straight away been suffocated by an intense feeling in my chest; and I've had moments where I've been completely overwhelmed and paralysed, thinking about the future and stuff I can't control, which I know now is anxiety.

I have grieved hard since Tin's departure. A year on I was still grief-stricken some days. There were days when I found it hard to leave the house. My self-worth is nowhere to be found on these days. But nearly two years on, I am really proud of where I am and I honestly feel really happy within myself.

What I know to be true for myself also is that healing can be a total pain in the arse. It can be unpredictable. It can be slow. Healing can be two steps forward then one step back. Sometimes two steps forward and two steps back. And it can feel like you are getting nowhere.

But I think you can practise 'acceptance'. It can help – a lot.

In *The Body Keeps Score*, Bessel van der Kolk goes a long way to explain how we can never totally erase a traumatic experience from our life. It's always there. But what can be 'dealt' with via professionals are the after-effects of the events that trigger, in my case, PTSD, anxiety and depression. He writes:

> Nobody can 'treat' a war, or abuse, rape, molestation, or any other horrendous event, for that matter; what has happened cannot be undone. But what can be dealt with are the imprints of the trauma on body, mind, and soul: the crushing sensations in your chest that you may label as anxiety or depression; the fear of losing control; always being on alert for danger or rejection; the self-loathing; the nightmares and the flashbacks; the fog that keeps you from staying on task and from engaging fully in what you are doing; being unable to fully open your heart to another human being.

It's important to realise that every single day you get through, you are making steps forward. Sure, you have scars.

You will have painful experiences. For me, what I've learnt is it doesn't mean that you are weaker or less of a person for enduring these times that may bring you to your knees. I don't doubt for a second they have made me into a more thoughtful, compassionate, strong and grateful human being.

A word on forgiveness . . .

Some people say you need to forgive – not necessarily the person who has harmed you but for your own healing and to move on. For many this is the way to peace. For me, though, I have accepted what my father did, but not necessarily forgiven him.

But just because you haven't forgiven doesn't mean you haven't let go of something bad.

It's more acceptance of the circumstances. For me there's no need to forgive the person who harmed you. I don't agree you *must* forgive to heal. It's not the responsibility of a victim to forgive. There are some who have healed and moved on – and they chose to not forgive – and I think that's okay. I'm one of those people.

To have peace, you are not obliged to forgive someone who has hurt you.

Perhaps you can even be more at peace by not forgiving.

I don't hate my father but it is very hard to forgive him when he has no remorse and can't say sorry.

Simple life

What also has helped me a lot with my healing is simplifying my life. Truly going back to basics helps enormously. When you are dealing with the after-effects of trauma you can get so wound up and weighed down in the past it can distract you from actually living.

So this whole theory of going back to basics for me is acknowledging that the little things in my life can do me a lot of good. This might sound quite simplistic in theory. But if you are going through heavy life battles, trying to find some joy – or at least peace – in small moments really works.

How might this look?

For years I never enjoyed a coffee in the morning, or taking a breath with it. Now I always give myself that time. And not just a short period. Even if it means waking up really early in the morning, I give myself at least forty-five minutes of free time before my working day starts. I fill it in different ways, whether it's savouring my coffee, watching a little bit of TV, scrolling my social media, or watching the sunrise from my balcony. I've never enjoyed this time more than I do now.

Writing

One of things that has helped me immensely is to write down, daily, three sentences that focus on how I am feeling. Just three or four sentences every day. And it's amazing how much worry, frustration, anger and sadness doing this releases. When I do I have felt lighter.

Not long after I had considered taking my own life in 2022, I wrote a letter to myself. That's how the letter on my fridge, which I shared earlier in this book, came about. And it still gives me comfort and strength when I read it.

Kindness

This is something I have had to learn. I grew up in a brutal home. Sport in itself is tough. When I left home, I didn't find much support and kindness until I met Tin and Slava, so now I know the importance of it. I know being a caring friend is really important. Helping others and being kind is a form of healing, happiness, gratitude and self-care. It's important to stay soft and not to let things that have hurt us turn us into a bitter person, someone we don't want to be.

By being kind and nice to someone, you can literally change and save their life. Not just their day but their life. Kindness is the most powerful human quality. It has the power to change the world. I try to be the reason someone smiles, someone feels love and believes in the goodness of people.

Notes on kindness

- Kindness is giving someone else your strength, your smile, your generosity.
- Kindness is a choice that comes from having great strength.
- Kindness is the most powerful human quality.

- Kindness has the power to change lives and the world.
- You will never know the impact you might have on those around you, or how much someone needed that hug, smile, kind word, gesture, talk or message. You can literally change someone's life – not just their day but their entire life.
- So don't wait to be kind. Be kind always.

Help with healing

What I have found that assisted with my healing:
- Asking for help – it's been life-changing for me getting professional help. It's been so important and amazing educating myself on my own trauma reactions.
- Connecting with other people, telling people my story. It's important to connect with people to feel less alone – friends, co-workers, family.
- Volunteering. I have been volunteering at different shelters and with different charity foundations. It's been incredibly rewarding to help in the community in this way and gives me a real sense of purpose and of giving back.
- Practising gratitude. I am grateful for my health but also I really appreciate small things in life and often they are the most important, like a great meal, a good conversation, a beautiful sunrise

or sunset. Now I never underestimate how much daily positive parts of life can help me be calm.

- Practising self-care by doing activities that aren't about work but are good for me. For me that's learning pottery, getting enough sleep, setting boundaries on my time (saying no to things that are going to overwhelm me), limiting my time on news and social media websites, listening to a calming app.
- Walking in nature. I have found this extremely healing. I love unwinding on a bushwalk or by the beach. It means time to myself. The ocean, rivers, the sounds of waves – I find them very calming.
- Visiting animal sanctuaries. There's something special about connecting with other creatures.
- Practising meditation for anxiety and depression (sometimes, not always, but I am trying to get better at doing this).
- Listening to different sounds on apps – when I go to sleep or am travelling. My favourite is the sound of waves, and of rain. I find these very centring.

Mantra: For daily injections of joy, remember the simple pleasures you can find in nature, relationships, positive routines and giving back to your community.

13.

GRATITUDE

'Gratitude turns what we have
into enough.'
Anonymous

We often forget that waking up each day is a blessing and something to be grateful for. I think gratitude is the biggest and most powerful path to happiness. I genuinely believe there is no joy without being grateful for what we already have. The more grateful you are, the more beauty you feel and see. I have never been happier because I've never been more grateful.

As you know, I grew up in a very humble home. We lived in poverty at times throughout my childhood and youth. My father was motivated by money and fame, but I never cared for that.

After years of hearing about money from my father and years in the world of tennis, which can be ruthless and all-consuming, for a while I lost my true self and the understanding of who I was as a person.

So how did my thinking change?

My mind started to change because of Slava Bikic. At one time in my life Slava was actually a more important figure to me than almost anyone. There are so many reasons I am enormously thankful she came into my life, and one is that she was the first person to make me stop and think that maybe I didn't have to keep fighting fighting fighting, and that what I had in my life at that time was enough. I had Tin, I had his family, I had financial security, and I had my career.

But also, what I saw in her so clearly was how what seemed to be the smallest things in life could bring her joy. She was someone who constantly practised gratitude.

As you know, her life hadn't been devoid of pain. Losing her brother especially was a great tragedy for her and she quietly mourned him throughout her life. But she dealt with adversity with so much dignity and grace.

Even though she had suffered, I watched as she found pleasure in the simple but important routines she'd established in life and in what a day can bring. She was a devout Catholic and I would observe how she went to Mass every Sunday and had a coffee afterwards with her husband and family – and how this would bring her moments of happiness.

I had always been a grateful kid because we had so little that anything more seemed a bonus to appreciate. Slava reminded me of how to be grateful later in life, after I'd endured a lot. It was she who reminded me to appreciate the small things in life.

Today, I realise the magnitude of her positive example. Gratitude has played a significant role in my recovery; its practice has been a part of my healing.

How? Well, there was a time when I didn't get the point of walks outside, in nature; when sunrise meant nothing to me. Or rather all it meant was that it was time to grind through another day. If anyone remarked to me what a kick they got from seeing dawn peek over the horizon, I would think, why? What's the point of that?

But now I get it.

Practising gratitude

The pleasure we can take in these apparently minor elements of our lives has been scientifically proven. In 2021 a Harvard Medical School online journal wrote about how giving thanks can make you feel more positive, 'relish good experiences, improve health, deal with adversity, and build strong relationships'.

The article talked about two psychologists, Dr Emmons of the University of California and Dr McCullough of the University of Miami, who asked all those participating in their study to write a few sentences each week focusing on particular topics:

One group wrote about things they were grateful for that had occurred during the week. A second group wrote about daily irritations or things that had displeased them, and the third wrote about events that had affected them (with no emphasis on them being positive or negative).

The psychologists found that 'After 10 weeks, those who wrote about gratitude were more optimistic and felt better about their lives. Surprisingly, they also exercised more and had fewer visits to physicians than those who focused on sources of aggravation.'

For me it starts before the dawn.

Right now, since retiring from tennis, I've never been busier. In the last twelve months as I've been writing this book my schedule has been jam-packed. I am booked out to do talks and conferences. Never in my wildest dreams did I think I would be an in-demand motivational speaker. A decade ago I was barely surviving day to day, so to be where I am is amazing.

Most days I wake up and give thanks first thing in the morning. It might sound simplistic but for me it's really effective – that forty-five minutes I talked about, so I have time to take in the sunrise, savour my first morning coffee, and be peaceful. This means that finally I am appreciative of my surroundings. I've gone from finding the idea of being in nature a bore, to understanding completely why it's so good for our spirits.

Every week I write in my journal. I express what I'm thankful for in the week that has passed, for my life. I reflect on the entry from time to time through the days that follow. I look at it at least once a day.

Another thing I do weekly is to write down the three things I am grateful for on a Post-it note, which I stick on my fridge. I've mentioned just one of many studies to show how beneficial this is, and I know sportspeople, celebrities and people I've met at my talks who do this, and maybe also ask their children to do it. I encourage you to give it a go, especially if you're having a hard time; just three things. It will take you no more than a couple of minutes.

These are some of the things that you can find on my Post-it notes:

- My health
- Roof over my head
- My friends
- My ability to do work that I love and that I am passionate about
- My strength
- My ability to push myself to the limit but at the same time ensuring I have balance in my private life

I find this can transform my mindset. For example, if I've woken up and felt daunted by the day or week ahead, when I sit calmly and do my practice, afterwards I definitely feel less overwhelmed and happier.

Practising gratitude brings calmness and joy
to my mind and my life.

I think as a society, because we live such a fast-paced life, it can get very easy to be distracted by materialistic things, as well as stress, but if you slow down and take a moment, it can alter your perspective in the best way possible.

Thanks to Slava and her gentle guidance years back, as well as Tin's, I feel as though now I am living proof that how we look at life – whether we're always thinking of what we don't have, or whether we're thankful for what we do have – transforms our mindsets and that can genuinely lead to a transformation in our actual situation. It's all about trying as hard as we can to move ourselves from a negative mindset to a positive mindset.

When Tin left it was a particularly hard time. But, in a way, the silver lining of that relationship breakdown was the opportunity to really reflect on myself, on my life, the way I was living it. I was able to take the opportunity to say to myself, well, okay, Tin is no longer in my life, but what can I be grateful for? What *do* I have in my life?

Around this I can reflect that I have a small yet solid group of friends, who around that time took my phone calls every day, to hear me download my grief, my sadness, my confusion. People like Todd would check in with me weekly. These friends taking my calls during this massive loss were there for me, they had my back. I have good people around me, who are watching over me, looking after me, caring about me no matter what. For that I am enormously grateful.

Maya Angelou has a beautiful quote on gratitude, which really resonates for me:

The ship of my life may or may not be sailing on calm and amiable seas. The challenging days of my existence may or may not be bright and promising. Stormy or sunny days, glorious or lonely nights, I maintain an attitude of gratitude. If I insist on being pessimistic, there is always tomorrow. Today I am blessed.

May gratitude change your life as it has mine.

The power of gratitude

- We often forget that waking up each day is a blessing.
- Gratitude is a powerful path to happiness.
- I genuinely believe there is no joy without being grateful for what we already have.
- The more grateful you are, the more beauty you can see and feel.

Mantra: Gratitude is a powerful catalyst for happiness.

LETTER OF HOPE

Dear Reader,

This is a letter to those of you who are suffering or have suffered through hard times, or know someone having a difficult period in their life. I hope my words on the previous pages have helped you somehow, lifted your spirits, or have simply assured you that you're not alone when you feel so. I hope these words will be ones you go back to, which can lift you up when you are finding the going is tough.

I know that tough times don't last, but tough people do.

Even if you don't feel strong, know you are a lot stronger than you think you are in this very moment.

Ten years ago, I was lost and unsure of where my life would go. I wasn't well, physically or mentally. Nothing in my life was really thriving, but I pushed through this and told a story, my story, which changed my life forever.

You will know from reading this book that honesty, story-telling, fighting, speaking up and courage helped me to become who I am today. You will know now that these qualities helped, are helping me, to fight through depression, anxiety, an eating disorder, my PTSD symptoms and my diagnosis of traits of BPD.

I have done a lot of work on myself in recent years. And what I truly know now is that my life is no longer just about me and what I want to achieve. My purpose is very clear – it is to help other people who are suffering from the after-effects of abuse, trauma, domestic violence and mental health.

That is what I am about.

You will also know that it was not an easy journey for me to get here. Even as I was writing this book, I was dealing with suicidal ideation, toxic trolling about my body, grief from a relationship breakdown. But the point is, I survived.

What I have learnt from all the awful lows (as well as the mind-blowing highs) since publishing *Unbreakable* is that I tell my story to make a difference. I share my life to encourage others to seek help, to maybe inspire strength. As I said on the ABC's *Q&A* in early 2023,

I'm not out here hurting anyone. I'm the opposite – I'm trying to do something good with my platform and create a safe space and a community. I believe if you stay silent – that is you don't call out the toxic trolling or behaviour – they, the abusers, have the control, so I feel it's instrumental to fight against that and I will call it out and stand up to it.

I believe that our silence is their power and speaking up is taking that power back.

On survival and setbacks, I want to quote Maya Angelou again. She says, 'You may encounter many defeats, but you must not be defeated. In fact, it may be necessary to encounter the defeats, so you can know who you are, what you can rise from, how you can still come out of it.'

She also says, 'You may not control all the events that happen to you, but you can decide not to be reduced by them.'

_____

My goal is to keep using my voice to build a safe and inclusive world to help and inspire people.

_____

We have to keep talking about mental health and trauma. We have to destigmatise these topics and make sure that the next generation has no fear in opening up about what may be happening to them because it will save lives.

I hope to keep rising up. I have personal hopes and dreams. I would love to be able to continue doing commentary and television work. I find motivational speaking so healing but what matters more is seeing the positive impact sharing my story has on others. That's why I do what I do.

I hope to take my messages about recovering from abuse, family violence and trauma to the younger generation, to perhaps even deliver workshops. And, most importantly, to consider what can be done to better protect those who suffer.

What my own personal suffering has taught me is that healing can be found in the smallest corners of your life. What I also now know to be true is that hope and belief go together.

I learnt this first as a tennis player. If you're setting out to play someone like, say, the greatest of all time, Serena Williams, you can't go on to the court with the expectation you will be defeated. You must go into the match with belief and hope because if you don't have those two things then you have lost before you've even set foot on the court. It's the same in life as it is in tennis. Always have belief and never lose hope.

Often I am asked at my talks what my superpower is. How do I get through times that feel really tough and dark? My answer to this is belief. I truly think self-belief is what has got me through the most difficult parts of my life, and is what can help you to get through these times. Sure, I still live with self-doubt and I have talked about my low self-esteem. But I think they can sit side by side with self-belief. When I'm pushing through something hard, this is what I call on. I know I can be strong, I know I can give 100 per cent to fight through those moments. So I'd say the biggest strength you can have, and one of the best qualities, is believing in yourself. Because no matter how hard things get, if you believe in yourself then you know you have the strength to endure adversity and survive.

What I also know is that anything can happen to us and much of it is out of our control. But with whatever I can control, if something needs to improve or change, I will do my best to make that happen through channelling my self-belief. We must believe we can learn how to cope, build up resilience, so that when the hard times hit we are ready. Not perfect, but ready.

The future

I have spoken a lot about the past in my two books – so what do I hope for next?

When it comes to some personal goals, I want to keep on growing as a commentator, analyst, host. I hope I can continue talking tennis for many years to come. Hopefully there are more books in my future, including writing a children's book. I hope I can continue my motivational speaking far and wide to reach as many people, including as many women and girls, as possible. A dream of mine would be to do a TED Talk. I want to continue to be involved in the projects and charities that support a lot of the causes that are very close to my heart: the advocacy in the space of child abuse, family violence, mental health, body-shaming, disordered eating, trauma and social media trolling. I want to be an advocate for victims and survivors of all these things.

All this is what I want my legacy to be. That to me would mean the world.

As I say at the end of *Unbreakable*, if my story and my book help even one person, then it's mission accomplished.

I know I can't change the world but maybe I can change one's person world. If I manage to do that I will die a very happy person.

Ultimately this book, just like *Unbreakable,* is a story of not just surviving but also of finding the power to thrive. It is a story of hope. Hopefully it will inspire you, give you a belief that there is always a light at the end of the tunnel.

I want to thank my fans, my social media community, all of you who have supported me. Your support, kindness and love have got me through a lot of hard times. I would even say helped to save my life.

To my fellow survivors and victims. I have your back. You are not alone. I understand you. You are stronger than you think. You are courageous.

Remember, there is strength in being vulnerable. Never let anyone put you down; always continue fighting; never give up on your dreams, and most importantly on yourself.

Hang in there.

Love,
Jelena xx

ACKNOWLEDGEMENTS

I want to thank the team at Penguin Random House, especially Alison Urquhart and Catherine Hill, for believing in my story, first with *Unbreakable* and now with *Fearless*. Thank you for putting up with my drive for perfectionism and my constant phone calls to work through this massive process of publishing a book.

I want to thank my long-time manager David Malina, and the whole IMG family in Australia and worldwide, for looking after me and believing in me for more than a decade – especially when others did not. Thank you, David, for always being there for me, especially in the tough moments.

Thank you, Todd Woodbridge, for being my greatest professional advocate. Thank you for being my mentor, my friend. It has been amazing knowing that I can always come to you; I am honoured you are one of my biggest supporters. You have helped me believe in myself when I didn't.

My thanks to Darren Pearce at Tennis Australia, for your guidance, honest opinion and belief. You gave me my first opportunity in the media world, and my first chance to commentate for Tennis Australia. If it wasn't for you, I wouldn't be where I am today.

Thank you to Craig Tiley, for your patience, support, friendship and kindness over the last fifteen years.

Thank you to everyone at Channel 9, from producers to talent to the whole team working behind the scenes. You have all made my work environment feel like a family and I will forever be grateful for that. A special thank you to Brent Williams and Ben Clark for your belief and gentleness around tough moments, and making me feel so supported. Thank you for giving me the opportunity to do what I love.

Thank you to Tin for being the kindest person I have ever known. For your amazing support and love for almost twenty years. Even though we are not together as I write this, I will forever be grateful to you saving me as a scared and fearful girl who was a shell of herself. Thanks for walking by my side for so many years, for believing in me as a person and in everything we tackled in life. Thank you for enduring all the tough moments and uncertainty. I will forever be grateful. I will forever hold those great memories in me.

I want to thank Tin's parents, Slava and Borna Snr, for what you have done for me. You took me in like I was your own and cared so much for me. You have been there for me for almost two decades and given me love through the toughest periods in my life. I would not be here today if it wasn't for your nurturing and kindness. You shaped me as the person I am today and your important lessons will stay with me forever.

Thank you to my brother, Savo, for your humour, for your support and always being there for me.

Thank you, Herme. You are always so supportive of everything I do. Your pride and tears of happiness when someone compliments me really mean the world to me. I'm so grateful for your friendship and belief.

I want to thank Jessica Halloran. If it wasn't for you we never would have cracked open the door to speaking up and shining a light on issues people did not want to talk about back in 2009, and then for writing (and doing the most incredible job of writing) *Unbreakable*.

Thank you for believing in me. Thank you for helping me write this, my second book. I would not be where I am today without your help and belief and, most importantly, your friendship. Love you and your beautiful family always.

RESOURCES

Lifeline

Anyone across Australia experiencing a personal crisis or thinking about suicide can call Lifeline.

13 11 14

lifeline.org.au

Suicide call back service

A free nationwide service providing 24/7 phone and online counselling to people affected by suicide.

1300 659 467

suicidecallbackservice.org.au

Family violence

If you (or someone you know) are in danger, or if you have been threatened, physically hurt or sexually assaulted, call **triple zero (000)**.

Family violence can include many different forms of abuse. These include physical violence, emotional abuse, sexual abuse and financial abuse.

Domestic violence is never your fault.

If you think you are in an abusive relationship, get help now. You can talk to your GP to find out about community support in your local area. These websites also offer counselling and advice:

1800RESPECT
National domestic family and sexual violence counselling service. Available for free, 24/7.
1800 737 732
1800respect.org.au

Our Watch
Preventing violence against women and their children in Australia.
ourwatch.org.au

Salvation Army
Family and domestic violence
Offers advice on how to get help and support.
Salvationarmy.org.au/need-help/family-and-domestic-violence

Children suffering abuse
1800RESPECT
1800 737 732
1800respect.org.au

Kids helpline
1800 551 800
Kidshelpline.com.au

Mental health
Beyond Blue
Focuses on supporting people affected by anxiety, depression and suicidal thoughts. You can visit their site for general information and advice, call their helpline, or chat with a counsellor online. Beyond Blue also offers six free sessions with a mental health coach.
Visit beyondblue.org.au/get-support/newaccess-mental-health-coaching.
beyondblue.org.au
1300 22 4636

Headspace
A site for young people looking for information about mental ill-health, and for people who want advice on supporting young people struggling with their mental health.
headspace.org.au

Healthdirect
Government website with advice on where and how to get help and advice about mental health.
healthdirect.gov.au/mental-health-where-to-get-help

Mental Health Australia
Offers information on mental health information services.
mhaustralia.org

SANE Australia

For people with recurring, persistent or complex mental health issues and trauma, and for their families, friends and communities.

For advice on Medicare rebates available for mental health treatment provided by psychologists:

Australian Psychological Society's fact sheet: aci.health.nsw.gov.au/__data/assets/pdf_file/0009/257490/Medicare-fact-sheet-mental-health-rebates.pdf

Eating disorders

Butterfly Foundation

Free and confidential support for anyone in Australia concerned about eating disorders or body image issues. All counsellors are qualified mental health professionals with a background in psychology, social work or counselling. They also have specialist training in eating disorders and body image.

1800 33 4673

butterfly.org.au

Healthdirect

Facts and advice on eating disorders

healthdirect.gov.au/eating-disorders

ReachOut

For advice on helping a friend or family member with an eating disorder.

au.reachout.com/articles/how-to-help-a-friend-with-an-eating-disorder

Relationship break-ups
Headspace
Offers advice on coping with this traumatic life event.
headspace.org.au/assets/Uploads/Resource-library/Young-people/
Dealing-with-relationship-break-ups-web.pdf

Relationships Australia
Relationship support services for individuals, families and communities.
relationships.org.au
1300 364 277

Safety online
Esafety Commissioner
Established by the federal government to help Australians have safer and more positive experiences online.
esafety.gov.au/

Australian Human Rights Commission
Advice on cyberbullying: what it is and how to get help.
humanrights.gov.au/our-work/commission-general/cyber
bullying-what-it-and-how-get-help-violence-harassment-and-
bullying

Discover a
new favourite